BUSES

YEARBOOK 2002

Edited by **STEWART J. BROWN**

Ian **Allan**
PUBLISHING

BUSES

YEARBOOK 2002

First published 2001

ISBN 0 7110 2804 4

Published by Ian Allan Publishing

an imprint of Ian Allan Publishing Ltd, Hersham, Surrey KT12 4RG. Printed by Ian Allan Printing Ltd, Hersham, Surrey KT12 4RG.

Code: 0108/F1

Front cover: **Stagecoach introduced Routemaster operation to Carlisle in 1987 — Twenty years of Stagecoach Half-cabs, page 54.** *Andy Izatt*

Back cover, top: **The oldest Olympian in the Southern Vectis fleet awaits its next duty at Newport Bus Station along with three younger but almost identical sisters — The Island's eighth wonder?, page 68.** *Robert E. Jowitt*

Back cover, bottom: **One of the first Optare Excels, on its launch trip in Blackpool — A Look back at** *Buses* **, page 86.** *Stephen Morris*

Title page: **Newport in the golden age of Bristols and Nationals, the latter, like the picturesque warehouses in the background, now swept away — The Island's Eighth Wonder?, page 68.** *Robert E. Jowitt*

Contents

LAKELAND
LEOPARD

David Wayman recalls the delights of being a part-time driver for Ribble in the 1970s, working a turn on the Manchester to Keswick service.

'Sign on Sunday 09.16 for the Keswick "dupe".' That meant the vehicle accompanying the 09.35 departure from Manchester to Whitehaven on National Travel service 836, operated jointly by Ribble Motor Services of Preston and Cumberland Motor Services of Whitehaven. At that time, in 1975, both had been part of the National Bus Company since its formation six years previously.

On Sundays the duplicate bus and both crews would work to Keswick. They would then wait until the service bus had returned from Whitehaven, driven by Cumberland staff (the terms 'bus' and 'coach' being interchangeable throughout this account).

Oh yes, one of the exciting aspects of driving part-time at Ribble's Manchester depot was the opportunity to enjoy a day out like this, *and be paid for it.* In the company's decimalised time, the duty would end 13.3

hours later, at 22.35. Scheduled mileage was 222.4, including the three miles from the depot to Chorlton Street bus station and back, although on this occasion an unforeseen event was to make a small difference. Almost all the work available for part-timers was at weekends. Occasionally it was possible to do a weekday duty or part-duty. Virtually all work entailed a late-night finish although this was no hardship.

Following the vacating of Ribble's previous building two years earlier, the new depot, in Hulme Hall Road near Manchester's dockland, had been shared with another NBC company, National Travel (North West). This was an express-coach-operating concern formed in 1974 from a company reorganisation involving Ribble associate W. C. Standerwick of Blackpool and the North Western Road Car Co of Stockport. Hulme Hall Road had originally been the latter's Manchester base and, from Ribble's 1,200-

Ribble 1026, for some years a Manchester-based coach, was a Duple Dominant-bodied Leyland Leopard, here emerging from the gloom of Manchester's Chorlton Street bus station. David Wayman

The standard outline of bus bodies as specified in the 1960s for British Electric Traction group companies, of which Ribble was one prior to 1969, was produced by several builders and could be fitted with coach seats. In the Ribble fleet, Leopards so fitted were classed as dual-purpose (DP). One such machine, a 1964 Marshall-bodied example in the cream and cherry-red DP livery, is pictured here just after leaving Manchester's Lower Mosley Street bus station. John Fozard

strong fleet, 28 coaches and dual-purpose vehicles were now housed in it. None had any form of power steering.

So for this fairly recent starter with the company, 09.16 it was, on a sunny and breezy September day. What bus number? Ten forty-seven: a Dominant. This implied that it wasn't an Elite, a Panorama, an Alexander, a 'Red Setter' (a 'White Lady' now turned poppy red), or indeed one of the two Bristol REs. That it was a Leopard and painted in all-over National white was taken for granted. Next to find the beast, get a tune out of it, fill the radiator and make for the bus station to pick up my conductor and, well yes, maybe some passengers, too. The conductor, or guard, in Manchester parlance, was Mike Slack.

Until two years earlier our starting point would have been Lower Mosley Street, further downtown in Manchester and the location not only of Ribble's previous depot but also of a bus station that was open and roomy. This was in contrast to Chorlton Street's cramped and claustrophobic facility with a car park on top. However, it was a drive-through station like those at Morecambe and Keswick. Other stations on our route, at Bolton, Chorley, Preston, Lancaster, Kendal and Ambleside, worked on the 'nose in, reverse off' principle.

The service bus was 1071, an Alexander in red and white dual-purpose (DP) livery, driven by Tony Wilson and 'guarded' by Brian Lefley, a seasonal employee. Bob Pritchard, of immaculate appearance and colourful language, was in overall control as duty inspector or, locally, checker.

The guards segregated passengers for points to Keswick and directed them onto 1047. Boot lids were lifted for luggage. Passengers going all the way on the 'dupe' would pay £2.90 single or £5.25 return. 09.35 came, and our two-vehicle convoy set off northbound with 1047 leading. At first we mingled with local buses mostly in the off-white and orange PTE livery. However, there were plenty of older Leyland and Daimler front-engined back-loaders about, a few still wearing the red of the former Manchester municipal undertaking. Its operations, along with some 1,200 vehicles, had passed to SELNEC (South East Lancashire, North East Cheshire) upon the formation of that Passenger Transport Authority and its operating Executive on 1 November 1969. They in turn had been succeeded by the Greater Manchester PTA/PTE, formed when local government was reorganised on 1 April 1974. More recent bus types on parade included Atlanteans and Fleetlines with bodywork of several makes built to the celebrated and eye-catching Mancunian specification.

During the first mile or so, our surroundings were typically central urban and then, after passing Granada TV studios at an altitude of about 100ft, drab old industrial. By crossing the River Irwell we left Manchester (the Romans' Mamucium — 'fort on the breast-shaped hill', population about 460,000 at the 1981 census) and entered Salford ('willow-tree ford', 250,000 residents), both with the status of City and Metropolitan Borough. Within 200 yards or so we turned left to head west on to the A6, once the principal highway linking London and Carlisle.

Before PTE days, Salford had been home to some 270 municipal buses, of which 210 were magnificent early-1950s Daimler CVG6s with distinctive Metro-Cammell bodies. How smart in their rich green and cream livery! Reg Austen, Ribble's arch joker at Manchester depot, had worked for Salford previously. Descending Rainsough Brow one day with a Daimler of that type, by mistake he dropped it down two ratios instead of one. Next, in his own words, the fan took off and sliced through the radiator. That must have created a deafening racket.

The performance of individual vehicles of the same type could vary considerably. Ribble's fleet contained 38 superb Leyland Leopard PSU3B/4R chassis with the horizontal version of the 11.1-litre O.680-type engine and five-speed Pneumocyclic gearbox. New in 1973 (Nos 1022-40) or 1974 (1041-59), they were 37ft 3in long, 8ft 2½in wide and had Duple Dominant bodywork. Nos 1037 and 1040 were of 37-seat super-luxury layout but the rest had 49 seats, the most common figure for coaches and DPs. 1047 was by no means the liveliest of the 10 allocated to Manchester. That accolade belonged to

1042, star of the depot, which 23 minutes previously had shot out ahead of us to Glasgow on service 830. Its crew would work it to Penrith and then bring back the reciprocating Western SMT vehicle. 1042 would continue to the Clydeside city and return on the night service, 834. We would follow in its turbulence to Kendal, where the Whitehaven and daily Glasgow routes parted.

When 1042 was docking, 1041 would deputise and was nearly as good. 1022, 1049 and 1056 were lively, too, but 1047? Hmm, adequate, but not at all stressed as we rose easily through the Pendleton district of Salford (some two miles from our Chorlton Street start) and on to Irlams o' th' Height (3½ miles). Here we veered to starboard onto the A666, which ran north for 26 miles through Blackburn to Langho, although we'd stay on it for only eight. Now here was Pendlebury (5 miles), and we'd picked up no additional passengers so far. Leaving Salford, we climbed gently to 330ft before the dip at Kearsley, quickly reaching Farnworth, both 'new' suburbs of the Metropolitan Borough of Bolton ('village with buildings', 260,000 people), the third and final Metropolitan Borough on our outward route. Anyone waiting at Farnworth's Black Horse? Not today.

Here we were deep in the territory of Lancashire United Transport, Britain's largest independent operator from 1969. It had a fleet of nearly 400 in a livery of bright red. Many of the double-deckers were splendid Northern Counties-bodied Guy Arabs. The forming of LUT into a subsidiary of the PTE was only some three months away, with full absorption to follow in 1981.

On we strode to Moses Gate (9 miles), saluting the crew of a DP from Ribble's Blackpool (Talbot Road) depot, bound for Manchester on the day's first X60 service journey from Blackpool. We'd share the X60's route as far as Preston. Shortly we passed Burnden Park, home of Bolton Wanderers FC, and then sailed into the bus station at Moor Lane (11 miles; 37 minutes scheduled running time from start) where there were PTE, LUT and Ribble buses coming and going on stage-carriage services. The Ribbles were newish Bristol RE saloons and Leyland Nationals. On that 1975 morning, a fair gathering of Lakes-bound travellers was waiting for us.

Above right: **Five 1969 Alexander-bodied Leopards originating with the North Western Road Car Co were acquired by Ribble in 1973 and repainted from National white into NBC standard DP livery. Here 1069, always a popular machine on account of its unfailingly smart performance and which the previous day had worked the Whitehaven service, waits for the photographer to re-set the blinds before taking it to Bradford.** David Wayman

Below right: **Ribble's 'White Lady' double-deck coaches were of somewhat bland appearance but put in many years of useful work on express and limited-stop services. The writer frequently drove one on a Manchester–Kendal journey. In this scene, another of the same batch rushes through Bury on a trip from Burnley or beyond.** John Fozard

Mike and Brian sorted them out for either 1047 or 1071, watched by Ron Greaves, the checker.

1047 found the A673, Chorley New Road, 1071 still in pursuit. There could be no dawdling, for, compared with Ribble's X60 Blackpool schedule, National Travel express services were allowed two minutes fewer between Bolton and Chorley and three fewer between Chorley and Preston. We climbed easily westward through leafy surroundings to a barely noticeable summit of 475ft before reaching Lostock then industrial Horwich (17 miles). Here, down the short thoroughfares to our left were the former Lancashire & Yorkshire Railway works, built 1884-7 and used latterly for wagon repairs. But the names of those streets! Armstrong, Whitworth, Brunel, Gooch, Stephenson, Webb, Ramsbottom and even the relatively recent Stanier: a transport history lesson indeed.

Horwich behind us, we left Greater Manchester, with its average of some 770 persons to each square mile, heading northwest into non-metropolitan Lancashire, with its figure of fewer than 180. Such numbers may say something about passenger traffic potential. Here we were in the District of Chorley (population 93,000), made up of Chorley town ('clearing of the churls [free peasants]'), some villages and rural land. No more large conurbations now! Winter Hill (1,488ft) looked over 1047's offside shoulder as the needle touched 50 alongside Rivington reservoir. Next came the drop down under the M61 motorway and the villages of Anderton and then Adlington (19 miles). Soon we rejoined the A6 northbound, and within a few minutes arrived at Chorley bus station (22 miles; 1hr 4min). Here we encountered more Ribble buses and those of well-known Lancashire independent J. Fishwick & Sons of Leyland, whose services linked parts of central Lancashire with Preston. Its smart and modern two-tone green fleet of about 40 comprised mostly service saloons, which of course were Leylands, with a handful of Daimlers.

A few folk got on and then, still northbound, we undulated moderately through Whittle-le-Woods (24 miles). Shortly we flew over the M6 and descended to Bamber Bridge (27) in the district of South Ribble (96,000 humans). The railway level crossing was open to road traffic. Bamber Bridge Motor Services, another respected independent operator, had been taken over by Ribble in 1967, contributing two Atlanteans and an Albion Lowlander to the (then) cherry-red 'big fleet'.

Now came the descent of Vinegar Hill to the River Ribble at Walton-le-Dale (29 miles), virtually at sea level and where the A6 was joined by the A675, the hill road from Bolton. There were several pieces of history here. First, at the Ribble bridge in 1648, during the Civil War, Cromwell's forces had beaten Hamilton's 24,000-strong army 4,000-0 — prisoners, that is. Second, from 1915 to 1970, Walton had been the home of Atkinson & Co, subsequently Atkinson Lorries and then Atkinson

When passing through the Bolton area, for decades passengers aboard Ribble vehicles on express journeys could expect to see the vehicles of Lancashire United Transport. Here, a Northern Counties-bodied Fleetline does good business. David Wayman

Vehicles, builders of steam wagons and then diesel lorries, with forays into the manufacture of economical, nigh-indestructible PSV chassis in the 1950s and 1960s, to be merged with Seddon of Oldham in 1970. Third, from the road junction, we were running where the primitive buses of J. Hodson had run on his four-mile route between Higher Walton (Gregson Lane) and Preston, from 1913. Ribble Motor Services was formed in 1919 to take over Hodson's business.

So we pressed on to Preston ('priests' village', 126,000 inhabitants) and up through its Frenchwood locality, the site of Ribble's Head Office, Central Works and a depot. The lively 80-stand Preston bus station (31 miles; 1hr 21min) was just off the A6, and comprised a massive rectangular island with offices, stalls, refreshment facilities and such like, topped by a multi-storey car park and flanked by wide approach aprons.

Buses in the Borough of Preston Transport fleet used the west side, its 160 presentable Leylands painted a rich cream and azure blue in a layout resembling that of Greater Manchester. Other operators' vehicles used the east. A few of our travellers alighted but there were many more to board both vehicles, 1047 practically filling up. What with passengers' destinations to ascertain and their luggage to see to (Mike muttering about the content of lead bars within the cases), the loading allowance of five minutes was more than taken up and we scuttled out of Preston about two minutes down.

Back on the mostly level A6 we left Preston via its Fulwood suburb. The West Coast main line (WCML) linking London with Glasgow was a little to our left, and we wouldn't stray far from it until almost reaching Kendal. We passed under the M55 motorway, which our part-week Glasgow service 832 joined briefly to reach the M6. Quickly we crossed the boundary of the largely agricultural District of Wyre (99,000 individuals) and caught up a procession of private cars. Mike believed that their drivers had conspired to prevent us from making up lost time.

As the villages of Broughton (35 miles), Barton (36) and Bilsborrow (37) came and went, the occupants of 1047's armchair seating viewed the low-lying and flat, lush pastures of the Lancashire Plain to their left and the bleak Longridge Fell, Beacon Fell and Calder Fell to their right. We cruised over the WCML and then the River Wyre, and avoided the Garstang bypass (39 miles) by forking right onto the B6480. This took us down into the village, which was entered by way of a narrow and severely humped bridge over the Lancaster Canal. It was

Top: **An Alexander-bodied Leyland Leopard of Lancaster City Council pulls out of the city's bus station. Lancaster's buses were blue and white.** David Wayman

Above: **Keswick-bound, a Ribble Park Royal-bodied Leyland Atlantean, as with all northbound buses and coaches leaving Kendal, attempts to nose its way out of Lowther Street into Stricklandgate.** David Wayman

best negotiated at no more than 15mph, but I believe that at some time previously a budding stuntman employed seasonally at Manchester depot had driven his charge over it at nearly twice that speed. A female passenger at the back was catapulted upwards so far that she broke her spectacles on the edge of the luggage rack and was subsequently awarded compensation — and rightly so.

Two people were waiting for us at Garstang (41 miles; 1hr 49min) and we took them in. *Three* minutes late now!

Good heavens, at that rate we'd never have time to wash down a gulped pie with a quick coffee at Lancaster! (Oh yes, we were into healthy eating habits.) On we went, looping back on to the A6. Tony was just about pushing us with 1071, as indeed he could have done; it was a considerably better performer than 1047, but for interior appointment its Alexander Y-type 49-seat body couldn't match the Dominant. A 36ft-long Leopard PSU3/4R chassis with the same running units as our Dominant, it was one of a five-strong batch (1067-71) that had been new to North Western in 1969 and allocated to Manchester depot, where they all stayed following adoption by Ribble in 1973. 1071 could certainly gather speed like its spotted namesake, and Matt Caughey, another driver at our depot, called it the 'sewing-machine bus' on account of its idling characteristics.

Certainly, Ribble crews could expect a Dominant on the Keswick 'dupe' and an Alexander DP on the Whitehaven service, although occasionally we might have another type of DP or a 'Red Setter'. The latter were service saloons in all-over poppy red (so boring!), sometimes used if a changeover was needed *en route* and there was nothing more suitable standing by. Some DPs and 'Red Setters', along with earlier Panoramas that

were not of the Elite variety, had the four-speed part-synchromesh gearbox, with Eaton two-speed rear axle in the case of DPs and coaches. None of the Plaxton-bodied machines had power-operated doors, and I only ever drove them south of Morecambe. Once, though, I did have the first of our two 1972 Eastern Coach Works-bodied Bristol RELH6Ls, 1017, on the Whitehaven service, and what an exhilarating run it gave us to Keswick and back! There were only 10 in the whole fleet and, like the Leopards, they had the O.680 engine.

Oh, those Alexanders! One part-time driver (guess who?) would subsequently become closely acquainted with all five, regularly taking them over Pennine switchbacks to Bradford on the X12 and Sheffield on the X48, as well as across the Cumbrian fells to Keswick on the 836 — demanding courses all. On their Falkirk-built, steel-framed bodywork just about everything that could rattle did. 1068 was the worst offender. Heating and demisting equipment was poor, and a bar of soap (carried routinely in the driver's pocket) was usually more effective. Brakes seemed to be worse than those on any other batch. But all except 1070 could put up a spirited performance, 1069 consistently being the best. The Alexanders, rather than all-white coaches, were used on Whitehaven runs because Cumberland operated its part

of the service with driver only, and none of our white ones had been adapted for that. Cumberland's drivers were said to have asked for Alexanders.

Anyway, the A6 was somewhat clearer now, and 1047 managed to keep its tail ahead of 1071's nose. At Forton we flashed by the new Lancaster boundary (population 124,000), ducked under the WCML just before Galgate (48 miles), passed Lancaster University and then slowed for the city streets. Here we rubbed cantrails with the fleet of Lancaster City Council, which, following the reorganisation of boundaries the previous year, had absorbed the buses from the former Morecambe & Heysham Corporation. The fleet totalled some 60 vehicles in a blue and white livery — mostly Leylands but with some interesting AECs. Ian Roe, another of Ribble's Manchester drivers, had formerly driven the municipal buses of Lancaster (name indicating a Roman station on the River Lune). He recalled the handful of five-cylinder wartime Guys, by his day rebodied. 'Twenty-five mile an hour up hill and down flippin' dale all day long,' was his recollection. Not *quite* as fast as our Leopards, then, Ian.

We romped into the bus station with the lost time nearly recouped (52 miles; 2hr 13min), but those refreshments had to be taken at break-neck speed to keep within the five-minute standing time. Leaving here, 1047 deviated from the A6 again, turned left on to the A589, crossed the Lune on Greyhound Bridge then passed under the WCML once more. We couldn't afford to waste a second, as only 10 minutes were allowed for the four miles of busy roads to Morecambe ('curved inlet'). We were scheduled to be straight in and out of the bus station (56 miles; 2hr 28min), but, as usual, with a fair number alighting and boarding, plus luggage to handle, a little time was dropped. Right then, we'd have to make it up!

And make it up we did. Along Morecambe Bay we zoomed on the A5105, Humphrey Head Point the nearest spot on the far bank, six miles across the choppy water. Those interesting AECs — ex-Morecambe & Heysham Regent IIIs with Park Royal bodies converted to open-top — beckoned on the other side of the road. Ne'er mind lad, just keep eyes front and make your Leopard roar up to Hest Bank where it'll cross the WCML on an overbridge.

1047's chauffeur was keen to get back on schedule, although further road traffic didn't exactly facilitate this. Back on the A6 again, the line of vehicles zig-zagged through Bolton-le-Sands (60 miles) and on to Carnforth (62). 1047 went roaring through, under the bridge carrying the old Furness & Midland joint line from the WCML to Wennington. The headroom didn't seem enough for a double-decker, but it was. Road traffic thinned about a mile further on, so the Leyland horses were let loose to do their time-redeeming stuff, eventually. Passing under the WCML, we left Lancashire and were

then welcomed into a county more than twice its size but with a population only about one third as large. This was Cumbria, formed in 1974 of a fusion of the counties of Westmorland to the south and Cumberland to the north plus a large chunk of north Lancashire, this most southerly bit being the now South Lakeland District (95,000 souls).

The surrounding land was much more undulating now than between Ribble and Lune. By our Levens Bridge timing point (75 miles; 3hr 5min), where someone alighted, we'd made up the loss. Soon, the A6 merged briefly with the A591 northbound, carrying fast traffic from the M6 into the heart of Lakeland. We dropped into Kendal ('dale of the River Kent') on the resumed A6. At the bus station (80 miles; 3hr 17min), we emptied a few seats, then filled more.

With no time to spare, we moved off again and, because of the one-way system, passed for a second time along Stricklandgate, Kendal's main south–north thoroughfare. A road to the left led up to the Kirkbarrow area on a steep incline and was the scene of a future event. One weekday, a Manchester-based pair was crewing a Kendal-based bus on an afternoon peak-time Kendal local journey from White Stile, low down on the north side of the town, to Kirkbarrow, high up on the west. The bus was routinely 1266, a former 'White Lady' coach-seated Weymann-bodied Atlantean PDR1/1 of 1962, which the crew brought from Manchester on a regular working. There was no other full duty at Kendal on which it could be used, as it was the only double-decker at that depot not then adapted for one-man operation (and, indeed, would never be altered). Alas, by 1977 the old

Opposite: **Ribble's final delivery of DPs to BET specification comprised 30 Leopards, new in 1968. Here one crossing the River Kent on its way south out of Kendal shows NBC's standard DP livery — white above leaf green or, as in this case, poppy red.** David Wayman

Above: **The lush foliage of Windermere village provides a backdrop for a Ribble Bristol RESL6L with ECW bodywork working a local service.** David Wayman

'Lady' was well past her prime, and it was a struggle to climb the hill from Stricklandgate — about 1 in 8 at its steepest, with a stop in the middle. When called upon to halt at it one day, poor 1266 seemed unable to restart. With a high rear-axle ratio, first gear of course was not as low as normal and for a moment I had visions of having to reverse down the hill, turn around and keep in the lowest gear (reverse) all the way up! Conductor John Begg-Robertson made an unrepeatable suggestion about organising a push from the characterful female White Stile laundry workers, who were regular travellers. However, just then, at one more attempt, 1266 staggered slowly forward, and finally made it hesitatingly to Kirkbarrow in first gear. The laundry workers wondered whether it had enough petrol in the tank.

But on that 1975 Sunday, Dominant 1047 was eager to head for the peaks of Cumbria. Our Glasgows kept to the A6 for the gruelling ascent to Shap summit, but on leaving Stricklandgate we went up the A5284 for two miles in order to regain the A591; we would keep to this road all the way to Keswick. North of Preston we hadn't risen to more than about 150ft, but here we reached 450, a climb of some 300ft in the three miles from Kendal. Beyond this high point, 1047 would be gravity-powered for two miles, to the level crossing of the Windermere line, a branch from Oxenholme on the WCML, just before Staveley village (85 miles). Here we negotiated an awkward double bend embracing the bridge at the confluence of the rivers Gowan and Kent. The spot was known to Manchester crews as Mason's Dip, in honour of the driver who tried to take his DP for a drink of river water, demolishing a fence in the process.

On the A591's switchback with some sharp rises, 1047 had to be dropped down a time or two. In order to minimise loss of road speed and to avoid any hint of a jerk or snatch, it was best to make 'racing changes'. The drill was as follows:

1. Watch speedo needle until it falls to several mph above maximum road speed for gear to be selected (50 in fourth, 33 in third, 18 in second; changing to first was never necessary);
2. Move lever from gear already engaged to neutral, with accelerator pedal still fully depressed, to build up revs beyond maximum briefly on the 'run up';
3. Engage next gear, and by this time road speed will have dropped to normal maximum for gear engaged.

That A591 road gradually veered to the west. When 1047 eventually came to the top of the final drop into Windermere ('Vinand's lake'),

there was before us a stunning view of the village (88 miles; 3hr 39min) and its neighbour, Bowness, on the narrow 12-mile-long Lake Windermere, backed by a skyline of jagged peaks.

Here we saw the small white and green buses — mostly Ford Transits — of Mountain Goat Services (Taylor & Hudson), a relatively new operator on the local scene. The fleet did contain a venerable Duple-bodied Bedford OB of classically elegant outline. Some rucksack-carrying persons alighted at the village stop. We then veered north along the eastern shore of Windermere, England's largest lake. The road fell imperceptibly from about 200ft to 160 before Waterhead on the outskirts of Ambleside ('summer pasture by the river sandbank'; 93 miles; 3hr 51min) where it was always a tight squeeze to manœuvre a 37ft-long vehicle through the narrow streets. More folk left 1047 at the somewhat cramped bus station and we forged ahead again, to skirt the eastern shores of three more lakes before reaching Keswick.

But what an intrusion, negotiating a growling Leyland Leopard coloured an incongruous white through idyllic Grasmere's narrow streets (97 miles) and between its buildings of local grey slate. Ice cream tea? Local yoghurt? Sorry — another occasion, perhaps. No time to visit the remains of Wordsworth and his fellow Lakeland poet Coleridge lying in St Oswald's churchyard, either. (Where the remains of 1047 now lie, I do not know.) Another few hopped off at the stop here, then we carried on for a really gruelling climb. Mike could relax for the 13 miles to Keswick now. (Subsequently he would become a driver and would transfer to Clitheroe depot. But what a shock to learn of his sudden death in 1984 at the age of 35.)

Below: **The Bedford OB of Taylor & Hudson's Windermere-based Mountain Goat fleet dates from 1950, and illustrates why the elegant Duple Vista was dominant among coachwork for this model.** David Wayman

Above: **It seemed almost impertinent for a growling Leopard to thread its way through the idyllic Lakeland village of Grasmere. Here, a Ribble 'Red Setter' does so en route from Keswick to Lancaster on service 555.** David Wayman

Above: **Just the place for a paddle, that superb spot between Rydal Water and Grasmere resounds to the growls of a National Travel West 'Tonka toy' (better known as a Willowbrook-bodied Leopard), after National Travel West had replaced Ribble as the Manchester-end partner on service 836 in 1977.** David Wayman

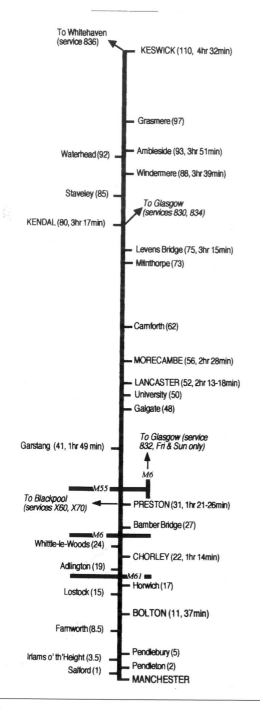

Manchester - Keswick
Diagram of route 836 in 1975

Main interchange points in CAPITALS.
Other stops in lower case.
Other Ribble Manchester services in *italics*.
Mileages and scheduled timings from
Manchester in brackets.

To Whitehaven (service 836)
KESWICK (110, 4hr 32min)
Grasmere (97)
Waterhead (92)
Ambleside (93, 3hr 51min)
Windermere (88, 3hr 39min)
Staveley (85)
To Glasgow (services 830, 834)
KENDAL (80, 3hr 17min)
Levens Bridge (75, 3hr 15min)
Milnthorpe (73)
Carnforth (62)
MORECAMBE (56, 2hr 28min)
LANCASTER (52, 2hr 13-18min)
University (50)
Galgate (48)
To Glasgow (service 832, Fri & Sun only)
M6
Garstang (41, 1hr 49min)
M55
To Blackpool (services X60, X70)
PRESTON (31, 1hr 21-26min)
Bamber Bridge (27)
M6
Whittle-le-Woods (24)
CHORLEY (22, 1hr 14min)
Adlington (19)
M61
Horwich (17)
Lostock (15)
BOLTON (11, 37min)
Farnworth (8.5)
Pendlebury (5)
Irlams o' th'Height (3.5)
Pendleton (2)
Salford (1)
MANCHESTER

Back on the A591, we set about Dunmail Raise — an ascent to nearly 800ft within 2½ miles of Grasmere's centre at only 200ft. For most of the way up, a Leopard would be down to 18mph in second every time. 1047 took it moderately, although on future occasions four of the Alexanders would almost be asking their driver to change up. Not 1070; no, it would thump its way to the top reluctantly in a manner worthy of any forward-engined Bristol K or L blessed with a rigidly-mounted five-cylinder Gardner. Driver Eddie Bibby attributed the uncharacteristic noise and vibration of 1070 to 'oval bearings'. It would take an overhaul to improve matters.

Our 680 engine found relief in crossing the old Westmorland/Cumberland county boundary — lately become the line between the districts of South Lakeland and Allerdale (96,000 souls) — for this marked the summit. The gradients were mostly favourable from here, and 1047 flew on. Nearly there now! The pleasant three hours in Keswick and the return journey, to be non-stop between Windermere and Bolton via the A591, M6 and M61, would make another tale. But what was this at Dale Bottom? It was a new Eastern Scottish Alexander-bodied Seddon Pennine VII on service 931 (Blackpool–Edinburgh), stationary in a dip. The agitated conductor indicated a clutch failure, 'an' it's got less than two thousan' mile on the clock!' That wouldn't have happened with a Leyland. Well, maybe not, but he didn't want us to take his passengers into Keswick as his driver had gone to phone for assistance from the Cumberland depot there. The problem for any rescuing bus approaching from Keswick would lie in finding a suitable place to turn. On that fairly narrow road there were only tight, gated farm entrances in the vicinity, and on full lock those Dominants had a rear outswing of about 2ft. I didn't envy the poor bloke having to do the job. OK, on we went, down the dramatic plunge, with parts as steep as 1 in 7 and a 'devil's elbow' just before the end, into Keswick ('cheese farm'), reaching the bus station (110 miles; 4hr 32min) a couple of minutes early.

Here 1047 began to empty as 1071 positioned itself for the final 29 miles to Whitehaven via Cockermouth and Workington, in the hands of a Cumberland driver. Yet before you could say 'yan, tyan, tethera', out came the Cumberland checker with a plea to 1047's pilot. 'An Eastern Scottish has broken down at Dale Bottom,' he sighed. 'Could you take your bus out and....?'

Left: **For some years, passengers arriving at Keswick bus station could expect to see Cumberland Leyland Nationals like this example, waiting to leave on the 14.55 departure to Penrith.** David Wayman

Below: **Of the same batch as the immobilised vehicle encountered by the writer on his journey to Keswick, a 1975 Alexander-bodied Seddon Pennine VII in the Eastern Scottish fleet, seen safely back on home ground in Edinburgh.** David Wayman

MADEIRA

'Rich, strong and fortified' is the dictionary description of Madeira wine. Stewart J. Brown argues that the first two at least apply to Madeira's buses too. He visited the island in 2000.

Above: **While the sound of AEC engines has almost disappeared from Britain's roads, this is not so in Madeira, where a number of late-1970s AEC-UTICs still operate. This SAM example is seen leaving Machico. AEC-UTICs of this style are typically dual-door 63-seaters with 3+2 seating.**

Right: **After AEC was closed, Leyland supplied units to UTIC for a short period in the early 1980s. The basic body structure was little changed, but the front end was modernised. This is another SAM coach.**

HORÁRIOS DO FUNCHAL
Transportes Públicos, S.A.

MINI GUIA
Transportes
Públicos Urbanos

FUNCHAL   Janeiro 2000

Left: Funchal-based coach operator Sao Roque do Faial has a fleet which includes Scania K-series chassis with UTIC bodies. The frontal treatment is vaguely reminiscent of the mid-1980s Duple Caribbean II.

Below: As Leyland entered its mid-1980s trauma, UTIC turned to other European builders, including DAF, Scania and Volvo. This is a DAF on the main seafront road in Funchal. There are also some generally similar Volvo B10Ms serving the town.

GROWING UP
IN CROYDON

Michael H. C. Baker looks back.

There is a danger, as one gets older, of looking back and believing the past to be better than it was, a golden time where each day offered the prospect of unalloyed delights. This is unlikely to be true. Almost my earliest memory is of sitting under the big, dark brown kitchen table and saying to my mother: 'It's 1940 now, isn't it ?'

Eight months later, just after my third birthday, the Battle of Britain would be fought above our heads. It was certainly exciting, occasionally terrifying. But golden? No.

Memories play tricks. This is an account of the buses, the trolleybuses, the coaches and the trams I grew up with and travelled upon in Croydon in the 1940s and 1950s. I remember it all with crystal clarity; or so I thought until I checked up years — no, decades — later and discovered that some of the assumptions I had made and would have sworn by were wildly off-target — simple childhood fantasies.

So this account is tempered by subsequent research and, hopefully, is therefore reasonably accurate — here and there. For I'm still tempted to believe that petrol-engined buses were much noisier than diesel ones.

It was a period of great variety. Three

bus routes passed the top of our not very long road, another the bottom; three tram routes also passed the top and there was a trolleybus route not very far away. Once the war was over, the three 'top' bus and tram routes were joined by five Green Line services, whilst the solitary 'bottom' bus route found itself in the exalted company of Leyland coaches in the beautiful two shades of green and pale yellow Southdown livery of blessed memory.

Right from the start I had no problem distinguishing the various types of buses, for they fell neatly into the same two categories as hymns at St Saviour's Church, West Croydon, where my Uncle Harry was People's Churchwarden — Ancient and Modern.

Ancient buses worked routes 59, 59B and 115, modern ones the 59A. Ancient sounded quite different from Modern. The former had petrol engines and rasped, whined and sometimes back-fired; the latter, with oil engines, purred. Much, much later I discovered that petrol-engined

A 'Feltham' tram passes Thornton Heath Pond in 1951, in the company of a Standard Flying 8.
Alan B. Cross

buses were just as smooth-running and often quieter than oil, or diesel, and the latter could vibrate unpleasantly. But these were not my infant impressions. Ancient were STs and the Tilling and original LGOC versions of the STL; Modern were the standard London Transport STLs. I preferred the Modern, admiring their smooth curvaceous exteriors, just as I preferred the similarly endowed (if slightly sulky) Pamela, one of the senior girls at my preparatory school, to her jollier but less æsthetically perfect friend, Peggy.

I lived in the area of Thornton Heath known as the Pond. The weekday 59 and the 59B terminated here, the drivers and conductors often to be found leaning against the railings surrounding the pond, drawing on a cigarette. Once it had been used to water the horses belonging to the charcoal carriers who had come down Colliers Water Lane from the Great North Wood — Norwood. Two main roads diverged at the Pond. The original London to Brighton road continued on past the tram depot, the top of our road and so to Croydon, while the other, the new A23, had been built to by-pass Croydon and rejoined the old road at Purley. It ran past the end of our road, across Mitcham Road (served by the 630 trolleybus), on over the West Croydon to Wimbledon railway line (now part of Tramlink), through the aromatic gas works, briefly accommodated the 403, 408 and 470 Country Bus routes, crossed Croydon's other trolleybus route (the 654), and then, climbing southwards, came to an open-air swimming pool (closed for the duration of the war) and Croydon Airport (formerly London Airport, and now taken over by the RAF). Beyond this was very nearly open country, before the road dropped down to Purley. Here was the terminus of the 16 and 18 tram routes, which ran through Croydon, past our road, and all the way to the Embankment. The A23 Brighton and A22 Eastbourne roads split at Purley, both continuing southwards towards the rural fastness of Surrey where green buses reigned supreme.

The buses which passed our road lived, chiefly, in three garages: Croydon, Streatham and Sutton. Croydon had been a Thomas Tilling garage, hence its code, TC. The other Tilling garages were the nearby Bromley, TB, and Lewisham, or Catford, TL. Both worked routes which served Croydon, but, curiously, no Croydon route served either Bromley or Catford, although the 12 got close. Tilling, of course, is one of the oldest names in the public

AEC Regent ST1 working from South Croydon garage on the 12.
D. W. K. Jones

transport business, and its buses honoured this tradition, being elderly in the extreme.

By 1933, when London Transport came into being, Tilling was tied in closely with the LGOC, and the latter was actually the legal owner of some of the Tilling-liveried buses. Like 'the General', it operated both STs and STLs. They were, however, not much alike in appearance, being outdated and rather ungainly. The STs had open staircases, while the STLs, although more rounded and fully enclosed, still managed to look old-fashioned, not least because their front upper-deck windows were divided into no fewer than three sections.

In the 1930s 10 years was considered a reasonable lifespan for a bus, and the Tilling STs were on the point of being withdrawn and sent for scrap when war broke out. They, like many of their LGOC-built contemporaries, were indeed withdrawn, but the possibility of untold havoc wreaked by the expected aerial *Blitzkrieg* meant that they were carefully stored instead of being scrapped. Many were evacuated to the provinces, and consequently I can only recall one journey in a Tilling ST, although their STL brethren were commonplace and regularly took me to and from school.

Croydon garage was destroyed, in one of the very last raids of the Blitz, early in the morning of Saturday 10 May 1941. It was not something of which I was immediately aware, for we had evacuated ourselves to the Sussex coast, east of Bognor Regis, where oil-engined Southdown Titans were the norm. There could hardly have been a greater contrast between the melodious Leyland

Services were, of course, severely disrupted that weekend but by Monday were almost back to normal, with Tilling- and General-type STs drafted in as replacements.

That summer we returned to Thornton Heath. Nothing much seemed to have changed. I was still sometimes roused from my bed by my parents in the middle of the night and taken under the stairs or down to the Anderson shelter at the bottom of the garden (I wonder how they decided which?), but the raids grew less frequent and life resumed its normal wartime routine. I had a few, random Hornby 'O'-gauge wagons, carriages and pieces of track, and one engine, but no Dinky Toys; additions were out of the question, metal toys having quite disappeared. In the sack at the foot of my bed on Christmas morning, 1941, I found an impressive (if rather primitive) forward-control, wooden double-deck bus. It was painted red with a white roof. The fact that some of the red paint was not quite dry led me to suspect that Dad had had a hand in its construction, and looking back I can imagine him, adding the finishing touches on Christmas Eve. Bus and tram services were still disrupted from time to time, and I once saw a smoke-blackened but still driveable 'E1' arriving at Thornton Heath depot. Buses and trams had the missing glass in their windows replaced by wooden panels, although I chiefly remember the mesh which was stuck on the glass to prevent it from shattering. There was a small, clear diamond in the middle so passengers could see where they were, but this didn't cater for less than full-size passengers, who thus resorted to peeling away the bottom corner of the mesh.

Top: **The LT-class AEC Renowns looked impressive thanks to their three-axle configuration, which increased their length and carrying capacity.** Michael H. C. Baker

Above: **The 'Bluebird' LTs were highly regarded by the author. One is seen bound for Mitcham on the 88.** Michael H. C. Baker collection

War was the norm. By the middle of it I had learned to read, and followed the various fronts in Europe and Asia with interest in the *Daily Mail* — it probably helped my understanding of geography — as well as the adventures of Rip Kirby and Blondie. Military parades were exciting, as were the convoys of lorries, tanks, long 'Queen Marys' carrying aircraft fuselages, and the like which passed down the Brighton Road.

purr and the AEC rasp or, indeed, the perfect match of the green and cream Southdown livery compared to the equally pleasing but other-end-of-the-spectrum London red and white. Four London Transport staff were killed on that fateful spring morning in Croydon and 58 buses destroyed, with many others damaged to a greater or lesser degree. It was the biggest single loss of vehicles suffered by London Transport throughout the war.

The sound of approaching aircraft could send a bit of a cold shiver down one's spine but actually there was little danger during the day once the Blitz was over. Night-time was different, and when the V1 'doodlebugs' and then the V2 guided missiles began to drop on Croydon in late 1944 there was real terror. But mostly I viewed my Thornton Heath Pond world rather like the bear who longed to go over the mountain, where he knew nothing was humdrum or commonplace. The rebuilt Croydon bus garage was home to the elderly and infirm, where other garages had sleek, modern standard STLs, imposing six-wheel LTs and even the bus of the future — the ultra-modern RT. Our local tram depot was no better, never playing host to a 'Feltham' or No 1.

Not all was doom and gloom, however, for these desirable items did appear locally, the magnificent 'Felthams' and ex-LCC No 1 working the 16 and 18 routes from Telford Avenue depot, and standard STLs from a number of garages, notably Streatham, which provided them for the 59A which, like tram routes 16 and 18, passed the top of our road. Elmers End was a garage which specialised in LTs, and sent them into Croydon in force on the 12, 130 and 194 routes. A six-wheel bus was highly exotic — elderly, perhaps, and essentially an elongated ST, but somehow more appealing than its shorter contemporary. This was hard on the ST,

but it had the misfortune to be the most frequently encountered bus in my part of the world and was therefore treated like an extension of the background — something that I assumed had always been there and always would be.

In fact, the ST was a most distinguished vehicle. ST1 had entered passenger service with London General in March 1930 — the first of thousands of AEC Regents which 'the General' and London Transport would own (although East Surrey had put a Regent, which would be absorbed into the London Transport fleet, into service in July 1929). Towards the end of its life, ST1 moved to Croydon garage and became a familiar sight, although, earlier distinguishing variations long discarded, it looked like any other standard member of its class.

The ST body followed the lines of the LT — the six-wheel Renown, which preceded it into service by some nine months — with the front of the upper deck set well back so that a canopy covered the driver's cab and the engine. This was certainly old-fashioned and meant that within a year or so, with the rapid advance in design evident in later LTs and then the STL, the ST looked distinctly dated.

At various times during the war, London buses were loaned to provincial fleets. This open-staircase Tilling ST is seen in Oxford, complete with a boarded-up window on the upper deck.
Michael H. C. Baker collection

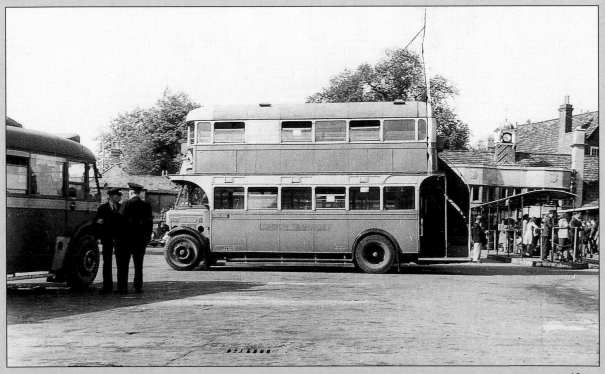

However, instead of the open staircase with which the first LTs (like the Tilling STs) were equipped, the ST had an enclosed one. This was straight and used up a great deal of space, which meant the ST seated only 48 passengers. The staircase seemed to me to extend almost into the middle of the upper deck and was apparently so designed to appease the Metropolitan Police, which at that time more or less dictated the design of London's buses and was still reeling from the shock of the displacement of the horse.

Perhaps another reason for my relative indifference to the ST was that there were very few variations from the norm within its ranks, at least in the Croydon area. The LT class, on the other hand, was full of variations, some subtle, others less so. First, there were the original, open-staircase versions. These had either square-edged or rounded cabs; I preferred the latter. They did not normally come anywhere near Croydon, although I did once see one which had strayed on to the 12. The rest of the class — the great majority — had enclosed staircases but varied in other ways, chiefly in the amount of information provided as to where they were going, and how this was displayed.

The upper decks of the later LTs sloped inwards, which added a nice touch of style. However, if it was all-out good looks you were after, then the final version of the LT, the 'Bluebird', was your baby. It was so named neither because it soared through the heavens nor because it introduced a startling new livery, but because of the colour of its upholstery.

The 'Bluebird' LT took enclosed double-deck design to its logical conclusion by bringing the upper deck right over the lower until it was flush with the front of the cab, and provided an angled staircase. These improvements allowed no fewer than 60 seats to be fitted. There was general agreement that this variety of LT was a real humdinger, the cat's pyjamas, and it is rather a pity that none has survived so that we can appreciate its handsome lines today. One got to feature in a glorious Will Hay comedy film, driving round the inclined banking of Brooklands (where, of course, buses of

similar vintage can still be seen each spring, at the great Cobham extravaganza). None was allocated to the LT routes which worked into Croydon. I saw — and indeed travelled on — my first one when I went to see Dad play cricket at Mitcham; as I alighted from a 630 trolleybus at the Fair Green, one of these magnificent beasts, based at Hammersmith garage, came rolling up on the 88.

The war in Europe ended whilst I was away again beside the sea — this time Bournemouth,

Top: **Unusual among the STL class was the forward-entrance Country Area bus, an example of which is seen loading at West Croydon in 1949.** Alan B. Cross

Above: **To minimise the risk of injury from broken glass, anti-blast netting was often fitted to buses during World War 2. An STL at West Croydon shows this, and the diamond cut-out to let passengers see where they were. Note also the headlamp masks and the white-painted edges on the front wings.** W. J. Haynes

A broken-down STL receives attention as the crew and passers-by look on. Michael H. C. Baker

where I got to meet real Americans (as opposed to those in the cinema) on their way to finish off the Nazis following D-Day, and yellow trolleybuses on which I travelled to school each day. Some of these had spent much of the war helping out London Transport in the Barking area, but, as that was far distant from my bit of suburbia, this was my first encounter with so surprising a colour scheme; until then, I had assumed all buses, trams and trolleybuses were either basically red or green.

Spring 1946 marked the return of both Green Line and Southdown coach services. I could remember neither from prewar years. Five Green Line routes, 706-710, now passed the top of our road, operated by those most handsome of single-deckers, the 10T10s. Their presence added welcome variety and some nice greenery to the otherwise all-red diet, although this latter is not strictly true, for wartime shortages had seen some trams and buses returning from overhaul in various shades of brown, which persisted for a little while into the postwar years.

Dating from 1938, the Ts were painted either dark green and white or dark and light green. The latter combination was the correct shade for Green Line vehicles, but many of the Ts had served as buses during the war (others were ambulances or refreshment vehicles for troops) and carried a 'B' suffix to their number, even though they were now back in their intended role. It has to be said that

Top: **When the war ended, 10T10 AEC Regals appeared on Green Line routes running through Croydon. This one, in two-tone green, had been demoted to bus work when photographed in Edenbridge in 1952.** Alan B. Cross

Above: **Variety in Croydon's buses diminished as the RT class grew in number. This example, with roof-mounted route-number display, is on the 154, which replaced the 654 trolleybus route.** Michael H. C. Baker

London Transport coaches were not in the same class as the far more luxurious Southdown vehicles, being really glorified buses with rather more comfortable (but still bus-type) seats, luggage racks and a clock on the front bulkhead.

Pleasing though it was to have London Transport coaches passing the top of our road, it was downright thrilling to have the full-blown 'real thing', in the shape of Southdown Tigers heading to and from the Sussex coast, down at the bottom. The local scene took on a very different dimension. At weekends, particularly sunny summer Sunday evenings, Dad and I would lean on the railings around the Pond, he with a pipe in his mouth, me chewing a section of Mars bar (sweets were still rationed, so a whole one at one go would have been considered not only staggeringly greedy but hopelessly spendthrift), and watch the procession of vehicles heading back from the coast. He would count Austin 7s, I Morris 8s, to see who would get the highest score, but I would also keep a sharp eye out, not just for Southdowns, but for coaches belonging to lesser but still interesting concerns like Orange Luxury, Timpsons, Grey-Green and Valliant. The Duple-bodied Bedford OB was the overwhelming favourite, although there were plenty of Tigers, Regals and Dennis Lances. No doubt there were still a few Gilfords, Tilling-Stevens and other lesser breeds, but these I failed to record.

Croydon had at least three coach companies of its own. John Bennett, whose coaches one boarded down a side road at West Croydon, operated a fleet of elderly, ochre-liveried Leyland Tigers dating from around 1930 but with later bodies; judging by the sound, they retained their petrol engines. I once travelled by John Bennett to Bognor, but I was much more familiar with Bourne & Balmer, which ran a fleet of considerably more modern Tigers and Regals (and possibly one or two Dennis Lancets) in a mainly grey livery. Its depot was in Dingwall Road, near East Croydon station. In 1948 I passed the 11-plus exam and moved on to Whitgift Middle School (where the Whitgift Centre now stands), just across the road from Bourne & Balmer's depot, and this company provided the vehicles whenever we went off to cricket, rugby or athletics matches. (If any of us had wanted to go to a soccer match we kept very quiet about it and found our own transport, for this was not the thing at all.) Then there was Homeland Coaches, just up the road from us. Its coaches were painted in a combination of chocolate and red; two in particular stand out, a Leyland Comet and a one-and-a-half-decker with a Mann Egerton body   both rare specimens.

Because the Croydon area sported so many time-expired veterans, when production of new buses got underway after the war we became

Left: **A 1937 Leyland, with Leyland bodywork, is seen at West Croydon. Most London trolleybuses were three-axle double-deckers of this general appearance.**
Michael H. C. Baker

23

almost *blasé* at the huge numbers of new vehicles which appeared locally. I write 'we' because in 1946 I had become friends with John Wadham and Clive Gillham in Class 4 at Winterbourne Primary School and received instruction from them on how to become a professional bus- and train-spotter, with the aid of Mr Ian Allan's *ABC*s, instead of being content with the amateur status I had enjoyed hitherto.

The first postwar arrivals were the Ds. These were Daimlers with Park Royal bodies. London Transport had already been allocated 181 austerity wartime Daimlers, but a further 100 delivered in 1946 were much closer to peacetime standards, with a complete set of route indicators — which were never put to full use. They were all sent to Sutton garage, and as one of the routes it worked was the 115 — jointly with Croydon — these buses duly appeared at the bottom of our road. The 115 was an odd sort of route, starting at Wallington, heading north through Mitcham to Streatham, turning virtually through 180˚ to follow the Brighton Road past the Pond and down the A23 through Waddon (where it was almost back in Wallington) and terminating opposite Croydon Aerodrome. It was later extended over the hill to Purley and down the A22 as far as Whyteleafe. These Ds, numbered 182-281, went into service in a new livery. Just

about every bit of the bus was red except for cream bands between the decks and below the roof. It looked all right when sparkling new, but I soon decided it was much less appealing than the old red and white in more or less equal doses, with a grey or brown (it had once been silver) roof.

Croydon's first new buses for very many years also arrived in 1946 and also took up work on the 115. Why this rather obscure, outer-suburban route should have been so favoured is a bit of a mystery. Anyhow, these buses were of purely provincial appearance, being Leyland PD1 Titans with Leyland bodywork. They were painted in a livery similar to that of D182-281, except that the upper-deck window surrounds were painted cream. This became the standard for London Transport until the upper-deck cream was abandoned in 1950, although no STs or LTs ever received it. Croydon also put STDs on the 133, one of its trunk routes which ran from South Croydon to Liverpool Street.

The 115 shared a fair bit of its journey with Southdown coaches bound for the coast; it was a coincidence that, around this time, that company put into service PD1s, some with Leyland bodywork, others with Park Royal bodies. Southdown double-deckers were regularly used as long-distance reliefs on busy summer weekends, but the usual fare gliding past the bottom of our road was the Leyland Tiger. Southdown really looked after its vehicles. Some coaches had gone to the military during the war, some had been used as buses and others stored, but all were restored to tip-top condition before taking up their old, intended duties. I could barely control my excitement when informed that the family had booked a day at the seaside in the summer of 1946 and that we would be boarding the coach at the Pond.

The great day arrived; we gave ourselves plenty of time, casting scornful glances at earthbound red double-deck buses and trams, the gleaming green chariot with its handsome Leyland chromium radiator sparkling in the sun hove into sight, Father raised his hand — and it sailed disdainfully past! Tears were close, but a lady in the queue immediately behind us, who knew about these things, assured us that a 'relief', whatever that was, would be along in a minute, and sure enough a second green Tiger came circling around the Pond and this time stopped. We climbed aboard, made ourselves comfortable in the high-backed seats, and, with that delectable Leyland purr which still raises tingles, we were off.

That said, in my insatiable quest for all things modern I have to admit that when we made the journey the following year I was slightly disappointed that it was again in a prewar Tiger rather than in one of the spanking-new ECW-bodied PS1s which had recently been put into service and had almost a monopoly of the London to Brighton route. To make up for wartime losses and with the growing demand from an increasingly affluent population which had little hope of owning a car in the immediate future, Southdown in the late 1940s invested in a large fleet of PS1s with a variety of body designs, although all in the company's beautiful livery looked very much the part.

We will end, where we began, back with London Transport. The Ds and STDs were merely the precursors of the bus which was to sweep away all others. I knew of the RT, although I'm not sure I knew what it was called, having come across it in central London, working out of the two Putney garages, but, one morning on the way to school, sitting on the upper deck of a 'Feltham', I could hardly believe my eyes when, heading towards us on the 115, past the block of flats where during holidays I sometimes helped the milkman deliver from his horse-drawn float, was something as far removed from anything pulled by a horse as I could imagine. Alighting from the tram, I ran up Winterbourne Road and into the playground, rushed up to Gillham and told him what I had seen. Pulling his *ABC* from his pocket with all the superiority which possession of this conferred upon him, he thumbed the pages and proclaimed: 'Ah yes, that would have been RT167, delivered earlier this week, the first of 2,500, so I believe.'

Well, he wasn't right about the eventual total, although for some time this was the accepted figure — until green-liveried RT2501 was delivered to Dunton Green garage in February 1950 and was seen passing the grounds of Whitgift Middle School, Winterbourne Primary having long been left behind. But the RT family would utterly transform the Croydon scene, replacing not only all the STs, LTs and STLs, but the Ds and STDs, the trams and even one of the two trolleybus routes. It didn't disappear from regular service until London Country RT604 was withdrawn from Chelsham garage in the summer of 1978, and, even now, preserved examples, including RT604, can often be seen on the streets of my home town.

Opposite above: **Typifying Southdown's stylish coaches is this 1938 Leyland Tiger TS8 with Harrington body.** Michael H. C. Baker

Right: **Although normally fitted-out as a bus, this style of ECW bodywork, here fitted with half-drop windows, was used by Southdown for some of its early postwar Leyland Tigers. There were 25 of these coaches, delivered in 1947.** Michael H. C. Baker

THE GOOD

GUYS

Four decades ago the late Harry Hay was active with his camera in Scotland. He had a particular fondness for Guys . . .

Right: Alexander (Midland) ran six wartime Arabs which had been rebodied by ECW in the early 1950s, and some of these were regular performers on routes into Glasgow from the Kirkintilloch area. One enters Dundas Street bus station in the summer of 1965; it would be withdrawn later that year. The building in the background stands on the site which would later become the city's Buchanan Bus Station.

Below right: Guys were popular with Dodds of Troon, one of the members of the AA co-operative. This was one of a pair of Park Royal-bodied buses purchased in 1948.

Above: This Arab IV, new to Duncan of Law, had rare Strachans bodywork. It operated on a service between Wishaw and Carluke, and is seen in 1964 in the ownership of Irvine of Law.

Left: Western SMT was a steady purchaser of Guys and built up a substantial fleet of Arab single-deckers; from 1954, when this Alexander-bodied coach was delivered, they were of the LUF type. The last new Guys for a Scottish Omnibuses group company were nine broadly similar vehicles for Western in 1959.

Below left: The last big fleet order for Guys from a Scottish operator came from Edinburgh Corporation, which took 70 Arab IVs in 1956. These had 63-seat Alexander bodywork. This is a 1963 view.

CHANGE AT
PUTNEY BRIDGE

Some things have changed at Putney Bridge over the past 10 years, while others have stayed much the same. Peter Rowlands has been watching the story unfold.

What exactly is Putney Bridge? It rather depends who you are and what you're doing. Often it's a sunny day, a light breeze and bright open vistas of the Thames, with the green of Bishop's Park to the north and boathouses for the rowing clubs to the south. In fact, if you're interested in rowing yourself, Putney Bridge is, of course, where a certain boat race begins.

If you're a motorist, on the other hand, it's a traffic jam. Going south, the next thing you come to after the bridge is Putney High Street — a major

bottleneck. Then again, if you're a commuter, Putney Bridge is a station on the London Underground. And if you're keen on gourmet dining, it's a trendy upmarket restaurant.

If you're a bus passenger, Putney Bridge is the terminus of a handful of routes to and from southwest London, and a stopping-off place for several others. And if you're really interested, it's a fascinating point of convergence for a variety of bus types. There's seldom a moment when you can't see at least one bus somewhere on the bridge, or one about to cross it.

Thread of continuity

For 10 years, the area has been a kind of second home to me, so I've had the chance to observe and record some of the intensive bus activity here, and experience the changes the place has seen. And there have been plenty. Almost all the routes crossing the bridge have had changes of vehicle, and some of the routes have passed to different operators.

Ten years ago, most of the double-deck routes were run by Metrobuses. There were even a few of the last Leyland Fleetlines, running on route 93 down through Wimbledon and Morden under the Suttonbus branding (remember that?). As I write, there are still some Metrobuses left, but they're running alongside a variety of more modern types.

Midibuses have come, gone and sometimes stayed. There are now two Dennis Dart-operated routes, but both of these have also seen Mercedes-Benz midis over the years. For a brief spell, we also had some of those smart-looking but noisy and troublesome Marshall Minibuses on the 39 (a meandering route between Putney and Clapham Junction).

The one thread of continuity has been the Routemasters on routes 14 and 22. Under tendering, these routes have been held for many years by London General and operated together. They both involve intensive services between Piccadilly Circus and Putney, but the buses arrive from central London via different routes (the 14 down Fulham Road, the 22 down New Kings Road). They converge to cross Putney Bridge, only to diverge again on the south side. The 22 turns right along Lower Richmond Road to Putney Common, while the 14 continues straight on through Putney and up the hill to Putney Heath.

London General was one of the slowest of the London companies to apply full fleetnames to its Routemasters. In 1991 they still carried the encircled London Transport roundel; then, for a while, a lot of them ran almost anonymously. There was extra interest for a time, though, when some donned Iveco radiator badges — a short-lived adornment reflecting the then recent re-engining of the fleet. This development means all the Routemasters in the area have a common sound — rather different from that of the Cummins-engined models you find in Oxford Street.

Opposite: **It's 1991, and an immaculate London General Routemaster is heading south over Putney Bridge.**
All photographs by the author

Top: **Remember Suttonbus? A Fleetline with both Suttonbus and (above the door) London General names nears its terminus at Putney Bridge station.**

Above: **Minibus services which have used the bridge include the 265, seen here being operated by an Alexander-bodied Mercedes.**

The station loop

Putney Bridge station, on the District Line's Wimbledon branch, is a couple of hundred yards downstream of the bridge itself on the north (Fulham) side. It's a high-level open-air station built on raised arches, with a modest bus station at its foot.

Above: **Iveco badges were briefly carried by some of the Routemasters fitted with that manufacturer's engines. This is a 1992 view.**

Several bus routes terminate here — the 265 from Tolworth and the 39 from Clapham Junction (both operated with Darts these days), the 93 from Cheam, the 270 from Mitcham. Other routes pass through, including the Routemaster-operated 22. But here's the oddity: through buses only serve the bus station on their outbound journey towards Putney, not on the way back. Why not? And why doesn't the 14 join in this game?

Go and stand at the bus stop outside Crumbs, the sandwich bar perched at the north end of Putney Bridge (and converted, bizarrely, from a public convenience), and watch southbound Routemasters approaching from Fulham High Street. The 14s keep coming straight towards you, but the 22s abruptly hang a left and dive off on a two-minute detour round the bus station. This is no doubt handy for commuters from the District Line on the way home, but no help to those on their way to work in London. They have to alight at the end of Putney Bridge and walk the few hundred yards to the station.

Since the station is on a one-way system, perhaps the prospect of having buses departing for two opposite destinations from the same stand

would seem illogical. And London-bound buses would have to cross southbound traffic to enter and leave. Nevertheless, the station loop is an enduring oddity of the area. It's welcome, though, on a summer evening, when you can sit at a table on the pavement outside the Six Bells pub (round the other side of the one-way system), and enjoy the remarkable experience of having Routemasters constantly passing within a few feet of you. If you're that way inclined, that is.

The green, the blue and the red

For much of the 1990s, route 85 between Putney Bridge and Kingston was operated under tender by London & Country, which used a batch of Volvo B10M underfloor-engined double-deckers with those large and rather ungainly-looking bodies by East Lancs. They became a trademark of the area, working the only frequent service not using London Transport red. Very occasionally they were augmented by the odd ECW-bodied Atlantean — a real rarity in Putney.

Then Arriva emerged as the parent of London & Country, and in 1998 put a batch of 13 new DAFs on the route — this time with Northern Counties Palatine II bodywork. So the London & Country green was replaced with the Arriva turquoise and cream. Then, amid the kind of advancing and retreating that has accompanied the consolidation of the big bus groups, Arriva pulled out of its Leatherhead garage and transferred route 85 to London United, complete with nearly all the DAFs on the route. And London United has since repainted them in its version of London Transport red.

Meanwhile, back at Putney Bridge, London General had acquired a batch of smart-looking Volvo Olympians, also with Palatine II bodywork, to replace the Metrobuses on the 74. This runs between Baker Street and Roehampton, on the other side of Putney.

At a glance the DAFs and Olympians now look very similar, although the DAFs are easy to pick out, thanks to London United's grey roofs; you can often see one of each, travelling in stately convoy through Putney and across the bridge. I've always wanted to catch a picture of the two types side by side, but I've never yet managed to get the shot I really want. I will one day.

Many colours

As a special treat for bus enthusiasts, every now and again the Powers That Be organise an extravaganza of non-standard bus types in the area. They parade over Putney Bridge and continue on to Wimbledon, several miles to the south.

Well, OK, this isn't really for our benefit. The buses are on rail-replacement service, covering for the District Line during essential maintenance work (usually on a Sunday). And I have to admit the appeal of these buses to an enthusiast is somewhat constrained. After all, they're not on a real service, and they don't all belong to one operator. They're a kind of aberration.

Given that qualification, you can't help marvelling at the

Above: **A London General Metrobus on layover, viewed from the platform at Putney Bridge station. The approach road to the bridge is in the background.**

Below: **An unusual type to find on the 85 was this ECW-bodied Atlantean which had been new to Ribble. London & Country normally used Volvos on the route.**

Above: **Putney High Street, with a Northern Counties-bodied Volvo Olympian, in 1997.**

assortment of bus types and operators you see represented — models never normally found in service in the area: Leyland Titans, rebuilt Greenway Leyland Nationals, Dennis Dominators, preserved Routemasters with AEC engines, even coaches. One of my favourites in recent years was a Metrobus from the fleet of Metrobus of Orpington.

The buses on these services seem to bustle along with much greater urgency than those on normal routes. So many to carry, so little time. They don't usually turn at Putney Bridge, but continue eastbound to Parsons Green, the next station up the line, running on a loop that takes in Fulham Road eastbound and New Kings Road coming back.

Diversion

Hammersmith Bridge, the next one upstream after Putney Bridge, has suffered more than most from terrorist bombings in recent years. For a significant part of the 1990s it was closed to all traffic but buses (only single-deckers were using it by then). This didn't affect bus movements on Putney Bridge, but it certainly added plenty of other traffic.

The bombing in 1999 was different. After this, Hammersmith Bridge was closed to all traffic during repairs, and that meant the buses which normally used it were diverted down Fulham Palace Road and across Putney Bridge.

It's strange how unfamiliar bus types stand out to the *cognoscenti*, but they do. These were recent Dennis Darts with long Plaxton bodies — very smart. But, in philosophical terms, did they actually exist or not? This used to puzzle me. I decided it depended on whether they ignored the local bus stops or recognised them and acted as if they were meant to be there. They seemed to, so I gave them the benefit of the doubt.

Above: **Routemasters lined up at Putney Common, terminus of the 22, in 1997.**

Left: **Marshall Minibuses appeared briefly in London. A London General example heads north in Putney High Street.**

Above: **The Palatine IIs for London General were stylish buses — and with good cornering abilities, judging from this example pulling away from Putney Bridge station.**

Right: **The DAFs allocated to the 85 were among the first new double-deckers delivered in corporate Arriva colours. The most obvious difference between these and the London General Palatine IIs was that Arriva did not specify a split-step entrance.**

For many years in the distant past, Putney was the highest crossing-point on the Thames, and was graced by a timber bridge with a strange curving alignment; this because the High Streets of Fulham on the north side and Putney on the south, although both leading to the river edge, were not precisely opposite one another.

The present, surprisingly modern-looking bridge was built in the 1880s, and, with remarkable foresight, the engineers designed it so that it could easily be widened later if traffic demanded it. It took roughly half a century, but eventually the widening was indeed done, leaving the five-lane structure we have now. And just as well: Putney Bridge is probably the busiest Thames crossing to this day.

The reason for that is plain enough: the bridge has to handle traffic crossing the Thames on several different axes. Southbound traffic arrives from Hammersmith via Fulham Palace Road, and is joined shortly before the bridge by westbound traffic from Fulham Road and then New Kings Road, in all cases travelling out from central London. South of the bridge, Putney High Street takes traffic off towards Kingston Vale and Wimbledon, while other roads immediately diverge towards Wandsworth and Richmond. Little wonder the area is so often snarled up. Unlike Putney High Street, incidentally, Fulham High Street is no longer a significant commercial centre. Many years ago the focus on the north bank switched a mile or so eastwards to Fulham Broadway.

Enlightenment?

After long-drawn-out road works in the late 1990s, Putney Bridge was left with a southbound bus lane extending right into Putney town centre. All very fine — except that it didn't help buses trying to turn right at the end of the bridge into Lower Richmond Road. It even posed a problem for buses going straight on, since the bus lane culminated in a left-turn-only lane at Wandsworth Road — not where they wanted to be.

New hope came during 2000 with the installation of an extra pair of traffic lights on the bridge itself, set back some way from the ones at the junction. General southbound traffic now has to stop here, while buses in the bus lane can bypass it, then swing sharply right — either to the middle lane for Putney, or to the right-hand lane for Lower Richmond Road. And it works! At least, it does up to a point. The only problem comes when stationary traffic backs up from Putney High Street (which often happens). You then find solid traffic all the way back from the 'real' traffic lights to the extra ones on the bridge — preventing buses from changing lanes, and completely negating the benefits. Ah well.

The new generation

By the late 1990s, the Metrobuses on most routes over Putney Bridge were looking tired and dowdy. Most have now been replaced — though, as I write, there are enough left to keep the flag flying.

By London standards, the range of double-deck body types on show at Putney Bridge is now surprisingly diverse. Just missing the low-floor generation were the aforementioned batches of Northern Counties Palatine II-bodied vehicles running for London United (the 85) and London General (the 74). London General's Olympians often deputise for the Routemasters on Sundays, and during weekday evenings on the 14 as well. If you want my opinion (and you probably don't), these are the finest-looking double-deck bodies produced in recent years. Also a shade too early were a batch of Palatine I bodies, also on Olympians, for General's route 93.

Alexander's new generation is now represented by a batch of ALX400 bodies on Volvo B7L chassis, acquired by London United for route 220, while Northern Counties' low-floor President (badged as a Plaxton, of course) was chosen by General for its 270.

All that's missing is the Dennis Trident: there are none anywhere in the area. So you'd get a rather skewed sense of what London operators are buying if you relied on the evidence you found here.

High tide

So what is Putney Bridge ? It's all this and more. It's the sparkle of water at high tide by the Duke's Head, lapping at the tyres of importunate four-wheel drives. It's football crowds after a match at Fulham on a Saturday afternoon. It's the Siefert-designed office blocks of the 1960s, with their marble facing now irregular and drab. It's the art deco Temperance Pool Hall that's now a pub. It's lines of spectators leaning over the parapet to watch the start of the Boat Race. It's the constant, restless flow of traffic, which never ceases even through the night; and the sight and sound of Routemasters on the 22, still plying the service into the small hours.

Above: **The Arriva-liveried DAFs ousted East Lancs-bodied Volvo B10M Citybuses on the 85.**

Right: **A Metrobus Metrobus on a rail-replacement service in 2000.**

Left: Buses for rail-replacement services come from far and wide. This Leyland Olympian with lowheight Alexander R-type body came in the spring of 2000 from the Wycombe Bus Company, at that time part of Go-Ahead Group.

Below: Stylish new low-floor double-deckers started crossing Putney Bridge in 2000. This is a London United Volvo B7L with Alexander ALX400 body.

ALL CHANGE
IN GLASGOW

Alan Millar, Editor of *Buses*, explores the recent history of Glasgow's bus operations.

O n 4 June 1996, an Emergency General Meeting of the employee shareholders of SB Holdings — umbrella owner of Strathclyde Buses, Kelvin Central Buses and the low-cost GCT operation — voted to accept a £110 million takeover bid from FirstBus, as FirstGroup was called at the time. This was the highest-value acquisition yet in the rapid consolidation of the privatised British bus industry, and the addition of SB Holdings' 1,300 buses turned FirstBus into the country's largest operator by fleet size. It also marked one of the final stages in resolving the shape of the bus industry in Glasgow, one of the country's largest cities.

Glasgow had been one of the first British cities to experience an all-out bus war when services were deregulated in 1986, but its origins went back to 14 August 1930, when Glasgow Corporation Transport took advantage of parliamentary powers to give its buses and trams a monopoly of street transport within the city's boundaries. Several routes stretched far beyond the city where they competed for traffic with privately-owned buses, but from that date the private bus proprietors were frozen out of the city market.

Over the next 50 years, many things changed. Most private operators were taken over by the SMT group, which later became the state-owned Scottish Bus Group. The city boundaries were extended in 1938 ready for a massive postwar suburban house-building programme, but GCT's monopoly was restricted to the 1930 boundaries, and SBG's Alexander (Midland), Eastern Scottish and Central SMT subsidiaries all served some of the new housing developments. GCT also gave up most of its services beyond the city boundaries in the 1950s in exchange for the British Transport Commission — which controlled SBG and British Railways — electrifying large parts of the under-utilised suburban rail network. Government policy also reduced Glasgow's population by around a quarter, with many families rehoused in five Scottish new towns; two of these — East Kilbride

The Scottish Bus Group used Routemasters as part of its competitive tactics in Glasgow. Originally operated by Kelvin, this one is seen in the city centre after Kelvin had been merged with Central to form Kelvin Central.
All photographs by Stewart J. Brown

and Cumbernauld — were within commuting distance of the city.

So even before anyone began counting the number of passengers who had deserted public transport for their first and subsequent cars, GCT was in trouble by the mid-1960s. Big chunks of its formerly captive market had either left the city, switched to SBG buses or were travelling on new

electric trains. In 1966, SBG offered to take over GCT's loss-making operations and rationalise them with its own. It even formed a subsidiary called Clydeside Omnibuses ready to take on the task. The offer wasn't taken up, and in 1973 the undertaking became part of the newly-formed Greater Glasgow PTE. The boot was now on the other foot. SELNEC and West Midlands PTEs had just taken over parts of the National Bus Company, and Greater Glasgow made little secret that its ambition was to do the same with SBG. The loss of profitable Lanarkshire, Dunbartonshire and Renfrewshire operations would have destroyed SBG's finances, and it was having none of it. Sadly, there was little co-operation between the two parties. Yet bus ridership continued to decline, PTE services lost money and the 1930 monopoly restrictions meant too many buses were chasing fewer passengers.

There was talk in 1976 of experimentally lifting restrictions on the Paisley Road West corridor to the southwest of the city and allowing PTE and Western SMT services to carry the same passengers and accept each other's tickets, but nothing happened. It wasn't until April 1982 that the monopoly was lifted and the long fuse on the powder keg that was Glasgow's bus market began to burn. The relaxed road-service-licensing régime introduced by the 1980 Transport Act had made such restrictions untenable. The PTE (by then

Top: **GCT was the low-cost subsidiary of the privatised Strathclyde Buses. Its fleet included this former Nottingham Atlantean, seen in Castlemilk.**

Above: **Strathclyde ran a large fleet of Alexander-bodied Ailsas, most with R-type bodies, as seen here in the city in the mid-1990s.**

renamed Strathclyde) and SBG were forced to negotiate a deal that achieved the Government's aims with the least short-term damage. Most SBG services began carrying local passengers, while many PTE routes were extended by short distances into new suburban housing areas. Such an artificial arrangement couldn't last forever; SBG wanted to develop its new Glasgow opportunities, while Strathclyde PTE was eager to extend routes to more-distant destinations, including the two nearest new towns. Each contested the other's plans in the traffic courts, and several tit-for-tat applications were lodged; some were granted.

In 1985, ready for deregulation, SBG restructured its Glasgow-area services into three companies — Central, Kelvin and Clydeside. With a mixture of ex-London Routemasters, new minibuses and an assortment of more familiar types of vehicles, it launched a new network of cross-city routes the following year. The PTE's bus operations were restructured as Strathclyde Buses, its route network was thinned in places, and other services were extended far beyond the city boundaries into what had been SBG territory. It was a battle many expected SBG to win. It lost. It also lost large sums of money, closed garages, sold surplus buses and may well have been hastened into private ownership by the drubbing it experienced at the hands of the dark horse that was Strathclyde Buses. The most visible sign of how far the tables had been turned came when Strathclyde replaced its rival on the trunk routes between East Kilbride and the city centre. To

prepare for privatisation, Central and Kelvin were merged to become Kelvin Central, and Clydeside was returned to Western Scottish management. When these operations were sold in 1991, Kelvin Central went to a management/employee buyout and Clydeside was split again from Western to go to a Luton & District-backed employee buyout.

Privatisation came later to Strathclyde Buses. A management/employee buyout finally got the company in 1993 in one of a series of deals that allowed local government-owned bus companies to be sold by closed deals, rather than offered to competing bidders. The deal had gone ahead despite some loud protests from Stagecoach, which had big ambitions of operating in Glasgow and had said that it was prepared to offer substantially more than the management and employees.

Stagecoach had, in fact, been operating its own Magicbus-branded services to East Kilbride and the large postwar suburbs of Castlemilk and Easterhouse, since deregulation in 1986. To clear the way for its bid for Strathclyde Buses, it sold this small operation to Kelvin Central in April 1992 — in a deal some suggest may also have created the dialogue for it possibly to acquire Kelvin Central at a later date. Kelvin Central had been steadily rebuilding lost market share by acquiring small independents in its area.

Glasgow Corporation had been the first Scottish operator of the Leyland Atlantean, and built up a large fleet of the type. Later PTE-owned vehicles were AN68s, and included batches with panoramic windows on their Alexander bodies.

Above: **Competition with Clydeside saw Strathclyde Buses serving Paisley, typically using MCW Metroriders on local routes and double-deckers on through services. This is a 1991 view of a long-wheelbase Metrorider carrying Strathclyde's 'Your Wee Happy Bus' lettering.**

Left: **Kelvin Central operated a large number of standard SBG Leopards with Alexander Y-type bodies, although these were being phased out when the company was bought by SB Holdings. This one had been new to Alexander (Midland) and is seen in central Glasgow in the spring of 1994, a few months before the SB Holdings takeover.**

Above: **Among the last new buses bought by Kelvin Central while still independent were 17 Volvo Olympians with Alexander Royale bodies. Two are seen in Kirkintilloch.**

Privatisation prompted Strathclyde Buses to create a low-cost subsidiary — or 'recruitment arm', as it preferred to call the unit — in August 1993 to operate some commercial and tendered services. This was called 'GCT', and its green/yellow/black livery, like its trading name, was clearly influenced by the Corporation and PTE identities which had been phased out in the early 1980s through the adoption of Strathclyde's orange and black.

GCT took to the road at the same time as hostilities between Kelvin Central and Strathclyde Buses came to an end. Kelvin Central city services — including some operated by Eastern Scottish since the late 1950s — were withdrawn, while Strathclyde ceased running in areas beyond the boundaries where Kelvin Central was the dominant operator. Thus Strathclyde pulled out of places like Cumbernauld, Airdrie and Dumbarton, but GCT took over the former Magicbus services to Easterhouse and Castlemilk.

Competition between Strathclyde and Clydeside lasted a little longer, but eventually ended with Strathclyde withdrawing its Paisley minibus services (and leasing surplus Metroriders to

Clydeside for a while) and GCT taking over some services through south Glasgow to the East Renfrewshire communities of Eaglesham and Newton Mearns. Clydeside also ceased using its Thornliebank garage in south Glasgow — premises it leased from Western.

By 1994, the Scottish bus industry was fast consolidating. Stagecoach bought Western, and British Bus acquired Clydeside and itself went on to be taken over by Cowie, which renamed itself Arriva and in 1998 re-launched Clydeside as 'Arriva serving Scotland'.

As Clydeside was negotiating its sale to British Bus, Strathclyde Buses surprised the world at the end of September 1994 with news that it was paying £11 million for Kelvin Central. This may have been partly a defensive move, as Stagecoach — having bought Western a couple of months earlier — is likely to have had its sights set on Kelvin Central and a return to Glasgow. Instead, Western set up a unit to trade from the mothballed Thornliebank site as Stagecoach Glasgow, running a series of cross-city routes with 36 new Volvo B10Ms and 24 new B6s. The first three of these were to start in November and December 1994. Strathclyde hurriedly bought itself some secondhand Leyland Atlanteans and Olympians and was understood to be planning revenge attacks against Stagecoach in Perth and Fife.

A couple of days before Stagecoach Glasgow was due to begin running, a truce was called as Stagecoach took a 21.7% stake in SB Holdings in return for Strathclyde taking over the Stagecoach Glasgow operation for the period before the registration could be cancelled. As a result, 18 Alexander-bodied Volvo B10M single-deckers joined the SB Holdings empire — with Kelvin Central initially — and Stagecoach's influence led to a fleet of 140 being built up over the next two years. This significant shareholder's influence also was apparent in the specification of lowheight Volvo Olympians for city routes.

By this time, the competition authorities were becoming excited by Glaswegian developments. While they appeared to have missed the end of the battles with Clydeside and Kelvin Central, the acquisition of Kelvin Central, followed by Stagecoach's shareholding, prompted a frenetic series of investigations and rulings. The Monopolies & Mergers Commission seemed less than happy about the first of the deals, but may have been prepared to tolerate it, with conditions. But the Stagecoach involvement was another kettle of striped fish, especially as the group had substantial east-of-Scotland operations, and the combination of Western and a stake in SB Holdings suggested it would similarly dominate the west. The Government was persuaded to order Stagecoach to sell its stake. Never given to taking such setbacks lying down, Stagecoach went to court and challenged this and a similar order to sell its 20% stake in Mainline Group. It eventually won, but by then FirstBus had bought Stagecoach's share in Mainline, and SB Holdings was also anxious to sell out. The price paid by FirstBus for SB Holdings almost certainly reflected Stagecoach's interest in buying the business and, indeed, was high enough for Stagecoach to walk away with a £15 million profit on its original investment.

FirstGroup, as the new owner soon became, wasted little time in implementing changes. It installed new Managing Director John McCormick — an engineering industry man with no prior experience of the bus industry — and started changing the image of the fleets. Out, from November 1996, went the separate Strathclyde Buses orange/black, Kelvin Central red/cream and GCT green/black/yellow liveries. But instead of a bright combination of orange, red and cream, as had been invented for FirstGroup's Leeds operations, in came a uniform dark red with, initially, grey FirstGroup corporate fleetnames of

Greater Glasgow, Kelvin and GCT. (GCT ceased to exist within two years.) The plan was to repaint or replace the entire fleet within 14 months.

FirstGroup also began to replace many of the older vehicles — the age profile of these fleets having suffered, like many others, in the early 1990s — with new, mainly single-deck low-floor buses. Stock-built Volvo B10Ls with Wright and Alexander Ultra bodies and Scania L113s with Wright bodies were ready around the time of the livery launch for the parallel re-launch of busy cross-city double-deck route 61 with low-floor single-deckers. This was part of a city-wide quality partnership struck to allay political concerns about the apparent monopoly which FirstGroup stood to enjoy in Greater Glasgow.

Maintenance problems at GCT prompted the hurried purchase of some Dennis Darts, including eight East Lancs low-floors which became available after Cowie cancelled some outstanding orders placed by British Bus. By mid-1997, 60 new Volvo Olympians with Alexander or Northern Counties bodywork were beginning to arrive, and would be the last new double-deckers for what had once been a predominantly double-deck fleet. They would be followed by large numbers of Wright-bodied Scanias, not so large numbers of Wright-bodied Volvos, and some Plaxton-bodied Dart SLFs, most of which — like the Olympians — would speedily appear in corporate 'Barbie' colours, as introduced towards the end of 1997.

Bigger issues soon intervened. As early as January 1997, one of the last acts of the Conservative Government was to order — following another MMC investigation — a substantial divestment of FirstGroup's Scottish operations. It was to sell either the entire Glasgow operation or one of the four city depots, which by then had absorbed most of Kelvin's Dunbartonshire services, plus all of the Midland Bluebird company, whose operations extended from Stirling to the west side of Edinburgh. It appears that, if it couldn't overturn this order, FirstGroup had selected Possilpark — its oldest city depot — for sale.

Within three months, Stagecoach came back with a bang. Perhaps fearing another player might beat it in acquiring the businesses FirstGroup was being told to sell, it launched another Stagecoach Glasgow operation, using new B10Ms and low-floor Volvo B6BLEs on a network of routes competing directly with FirstGroup; the cleverest were innovative urban motorway links to the large Easterhouse and Pollok suburbs. The battle soon broke out into a mini-war, with FirstGroup adding

Above: Under FirstGroup control a new and undistinguished overall-red livery was adopted for all of the fleets which had been part of SB Holdings. Originally these retained their names — GCT, Greater Glasgow and Kelvin — but ultimately all were branded as First Glasgow. This Gardner-engined Tiger was new to Central SMT and has an Alexander TS-type body. It contrasts sharply with the Dennis Dart in the background.

Right: The last 10 Royales for Kelvin Central were unusual in being of lowheight design. One turns into Buchanan Bus Station in August 2000.

Above: **Stagecoach introduced routes to compete with FirstGroup in Glasgow. A Volvo B10M with Alexander PS-type body advertises the company's Megarider ticket in its destination display.**

Left: **High-frequency services were given Overground branding in 1999, as seen here on a Wright-bodied Scania in the bus station at St Enoch Square, since closed.**

Above: **Strathclyde PTE's fondness for the Ailsa has left First Glasgow with a legacy of noisy front-engined buses — but they are being replaced by new low-floor single-deckers.**

new routes to its Glasgow network, and hitting back against Stagecoach in Ayrshire and Fife along lines SB Holdings had contemplated three years earlier. There was talk of these battles extending to Newcastle, and the Glasgow fleets later acquired some Volvo B6LEs with Leeds registrations.

If these battles did nothing else, they temporarily reduced fares and increased frequencies on major corridors, and created an impression that perhaps there was sufficient competition to call off the divestment order. After much lobbying, the new Labour Government conceded in July 1998 that FirstGroup could keep its Glasgow and Midland Bluebird operations. By then, all the former SB Holdings businesses were trading as First Glasgow, with Strathclyde Buses given the official name of 'First Glasgow (No 1) Ltd' and Kelvin Central renamed 'First Glasgow (No 2) Ltd'. The drab red livery had been brightened a little by the adoption of white First fleetnames in place of the earlier grey. It would take until the summer of 1999 for the last orange buses to be repainted, the programme having been slowed by the uncertainty over Possilpark, which was closed voluntarily in mid-2000.

Since then, Stagecoach has withdrawn completely from two of the suburbs it served at the height of the battles and has cut back frequencies on other corridors, while FirstGroup has withdrawn from Fife and has reduced some of its most competitive Glasgow routes.

The biggest event of 1999 was the launch of the Overground network, the prototype for (and, to date, the largest example of) the simplified urban bus networks introduced by FirstGroup around the country. Implemented by Bob Montgomery, the professional busman who had taken over as Managing Director and later went on to head FirstGroup's entire Scottish operation, this addressed two of the biggest complaints levelled against bus services in Glasgow. Few non-bus users had a clue where services ran. And once they got to know, the services usually changed. Again and again. And again.

The 18 mainly cross-city routes branded as Overground were displayed on stylised maps rather like those for the London Underground, and came with pledges of high daytime frequencies and a commitment not to alter them for at least 10 years; until then, 10 weeks without changes to the city's services had been a good run. There also was a commitment to convert many of them to 24-hour operation. As Bob Montgomery explained, these were the routes where FirstGroup would run trams if it ever got the chance.

Another side of the Overground story was that none of the publicity left much if any clue as to where the company's other routes ran, if, indeed, they existed at all. Nor were they cast in stone like the busiest 18 routes. There have been several radical changes since then, and one of the more curious (if understandable) by-products of it all has been that the 18 Overground routes have been progressively converted to standee single-deck operation (including 10 articulated Volvo B10LAs), while the quieter routes often run with the oldest double-deckers.

Outside Glasgow, the extensive former Central SMT and Eastern Scottish networks in Lanarkshire have been pruned drastically, with a host of expanding independents running many of the services provided for decades by SBG.

Although the big group battles have died down in the city, competition most certainly hasn't. Several corridors and routes radiating from local centres in Clydebank and Govan — either side of the Clyde, to the west of the city — are served by independent operators, most of whom use secondhand ex-major fleet minibuses. First Glasgow's introduction from January 2001 of higher-frequency minibuses in place of double-deckers on some secondary routes may signal the possible next phase in the story of the city's buses — a fightback against the successful independents.

Left: **Not all Overground routes got new low-floor buses. Here an Alexander-bodied Leyland Olympian loads in Clydebank for the long cross-city trip to East Kilbride.**

Below: **Minibuses have largely disappeared from mainstream First Glasgow operations. Those currently in service are Mercedes-Benz transferred in from other parts of the FirstGroup empire. This 1988 811D with Alexander body came north from CentreWest in 1997.**

HAVE A NICE DAY!

John Marsh turns to poetry, so impressed is he by a transport day out.

Where else but in a country shire,
So much to see, lots to admire?
The July sun, for once so kind
To those who history hope to find
Of public transport from the past
When days were long, life not so fast.
Of buses, and of trains as well,
Proud fathers to their children tell:
"I went to school on one of those",
To looks of wonderment — who knows
What thoughts the children had,
"You mean on that? How old is Dad?"

Such is the Mid-Hants Running Day,
Where men are boys who love to play
At running buses back and forth,
From Alton to the south and north,
Then east and west and back again.
To take the bus or take the train,
The biggest question to decide
On steam train or by bus to ride?

Down narrow lanes the routes explore
Where no bus ever went before!
To places where once meet you might
Jane Austen or Rev Gilbert White.
Whilst locals look in disbelief
"Is that an airport coach? Good grief!"
And what is more, the rides are free,
A Dennis Dart from 'thirty-three,
Or maybe, preferable to you,
A Trident in that peacock blue?

At Anstey Park in pristine rows
Bright paintwork positively glows,
Their owners' very prides and joys
These buses, are they big boys' toys?
Not 'til you've done the photocalls
Will there be time to view the stalls.
So for a mini spending spree
A Corgi or that EFE
You might have missed the first time round.
There's many a bargain to be found!

And when, at last, exhaustion comes
Thoughts turn to empty, rumbling tums,
Ah! Fish and chips for all of us
Served from an ageing Bedford bus.
And so, for home, the day well spent,
There's no regretting that we went.
Where else (can anybody say?)
Could folks enjoy a better day?

NORTH AMERICAN
MISCELLANY

In much of North America there is no public transport worth mentioning, but in the bigger urban areas there are intensive networks — usually bus-based, but in some cities supported by trolleybuses and both light and 'heavy' rail services. Stewart J. Brown illustrates a selection.

Above: **Providence, Rhode Island, is served by the Rhode Island Public Transport Authority whose fleet includes RTS buses built by GMC and later by TMC. An RTS emerges from the bus-only tunnel underneath College Hill. The tunnel was originally used by trams.**

Right: **It would take a sharp eye to spot it, but this International school bus is owned by FirstGroup. Seen crossing the bascule bridge in Mystic, Connecticut, it carries 'First Student' lettering on the lower side panels.**

Left: Niagara Transit, serving the Canadian town alongside the famous falls, still operates classic GMC 'new look' buses. Once to be seen in most cities in North America, this style of GMC transit bus is fast disappearing.

Below left: A tourist bus of a different kind is the DUKW, with a fleet operated by Boston Duck Tours providing visitors with the rare experience of travelling in an amphibious vehicle. The DUKWs have to meet both road- and water-related legislation.

Below: Another classic to be seen in Niagara is the London Transport Routemaster, which continues a long tradition of running London buses for tourists visiting the falls. This extremely smart example is RM1676.

Left: Electric buses are operated in Santa Barbara, California — the state most conscious of the problems caused by motor-vehicle pollution. Most are so-called 'replica trolleys', running on a downtown shuttle, but this is a real bus, seen pulling out of the town's central bus station.

51

Above: **Boston has an extensive and efficient light rail network. Each of the city's lines is colour-coded; this is a Green Line Boeing-Vertol dating from 1976 and wearing its age lightly in this 2000 photograph.**

Right: **The San Francisco Muni operates 60 New Flyer articulated trolleybuses delivered in the early 1990s.**

Above: Classic PCC trams are operated on a route along Market Street by the San Francisco Muni. These are painted in the liveries of a variety of North American systems, in this case the green and cream of Illinois Terminal.

Left: SamTrans is the name used by San Mateo County Transit District, running around 350 buses to the south of San Francisco. These include articulated models from Volvo, New Flyer and, as seen here, Neoplan.

Below: In Albany, the capital of New York State, the Capital District Transportation Authority operates some 230 buses. Most are Orions, but the most recent deliveries have been Nova Bus LFS low-floor vehicles. This one is bound for Schenectady, known to enthusiasts with wide-ranging transport interests as the home of locomotive builder ALCO — the American Locomotive Company.

20 YEARS OF
STAGECOACH
HALF-CABS

Stagecoach was created over a decade after the last new half-cabs were built for UK service, but managed to operate a surprising number, as Andy Izatt explains.

The phenomenal growth of Stagecoach over the past 20 years has been well documented. The business acumen of Brian Souter and his elder sister Ann Gloag has made the company a household name. There are many factors behind this success, but amongst the most important has been Brian Souter's ability to spot an opportunity and grasp it before anyone else. That ability paved the way for the use of half-cabs as a competitive tool in the 1980s and 1990s when most other operators would have viewed the concept as an anachronism. Although they had disappeared from most British fleets before Gloagtrotter bought its first bus, Stagecoach went on to run them in Europe, North America, Africa and the Far East.

Opposite: **FLF Lodekka HGM 335E, new to Central SMT in 1967, is still owned by Stagecoach as part of its preserved fleet. In September 1984 it was still in Gloagtrotter livery.** All photographs by the author

Left: **Seen at work in Perth during March 1987, this Lodekka was originally a Southern Vectis bus. In April 1992 it was exported to Canada to work for Gray Coach Lines, Toronto, after East Midland had converted it to offside-door.**

Left: **Stagecoach bought this former Northern General Routemaster from Stevenson's of Spath in accident-damaged condition. It was repaired and put to work with Magicbus in Glasgow, and is here seen leaving Port Dundas on a works contract in 1987.**

Pragmatic start

Three types have featured prominently. High-capacity Daimler CVG6LX-34s operated overseas and Routemasters throughout the UK, but it was the Lodekka to which the company first turned and remained loyal in the early years. While studying accountancy at Strathclyde University in the 1970s, Brian Souter worked as a conductor with Central SMT. It gave him direct experience of Bristol reliability and the values, economic and social, of crew operation.

Appropriately, for the fledgling Gloagtrotter business based at Perth Harbour, the first double-decker was a former Central SMT Bristol FLF6G, FGM 306D. It arrived in December 1980, the same month that A. & C. McLennan's route between Perth and Errol was taken over. It was followed in August 1981 by two more, and all three found work on contracts and the local service, and in providing extra capacity on express routes at peak times. One is still owned by the company and, although technically part of the Bluebird fleet, is preserved at the Scottish Vintage Bus Museum, Lathalmond.

Surprise purchases in April 1981 were a pair of convertible-open-top Bristol FS6Gs dating from 1961, when consideration was being given to a Perth city tour. The tour did not materialise, and one was sold after a year to Ensignbus. The other stayed much longer, although its use in open-top form was rare. In the late 1980s, painted white, it worked as a driver trainer as Stagecoach expanded in Perth at the expense of Strathtay.

By the time two former Eastern National Bristol FLFs joined the Perth operation in April 1982, the Stagecoach name had been adopted for all of the firm's activities, not just express-coach routes. They were followed by another six FLFs in 1983, with the net being cast far and wide for suitable vehicles.

Perhaps the most surprising purchase of 1983 was a former Alexander (Fife) FS6G acquired from preservationists. This bus was a regular on Perth-area services until it was sold, once again into preservation, in November 1990.

Irvine of Law sold two former Eastern National FLFs to Stagecoach in January 1984. Four Southern Vectis buses followed in the summer. Edinburgh-based Adamson & Low had been bought by Stagecoach in November 1983 and additional Lodekkas were needed to cover the new commitments, although none was licensed to that operation. The only 'deckers that were were a pair of former Leicester Leyland PD3A/12s bought from Park's of Hamilton. Painted into Stagecoach livery, they lasted a year before being sold.

Routemaster first

Considerable surprise was expressed when Stagecoach bought its first five Routemasters from London Regional Transport in January 1985. But Brian Souter knew a bargain when he saw one, and another five were snapped up the following May. When 847 DYE entered service on the Errol route in March, still in London Transport red, it

Right: **Typical of the Routemasters used in Glasgow by Magicbus, 607 DYE approaches St Enoch from Castlemilk in April 1987.**

Below: **The ex-McLennan's Massey-bodied Daimler CCG5 on which Brian Souter passed his PSV driving test, parked at Walnut Grove in April 1987. It later returned to its home town of Burton-upon-Trent for restoration.**

Stagecoach's growing local commitments warranted the purchase of three FLF6Gs from Kinross Investments in February 1986, while another was acquired from Cramlington-based Target Travel for spares. Many longer-serving Lodekkas from the operational fleet suffered a similar fate. Often they were dumped in the field next to Spittalfield garage, along with other withdrawn vehicles, continuing a long-standing McLennan's tradition.

The Stagecoach cheque book strayed to Wales in the summer, with FLFs coming from Eagles & Hughes of Mold, Silcox of Pembroke Dock and Cleverly of Cwmbran. Nearer to home, local farmer Petrie of Longforgan was the source of a former Lincolnshire Bristol FS5G. Although its bodywork was extensively refurbished, it did not enter service with Stagecoach and was sold five years later after a mechanical overhaul, complete with a Class V ticket.

made history as the first Scottish Routemaster. Reflecting that windchill temperatures in rural Scotland can be noticeably lower than in central London, sister 611 DYE had rear doors fitted in April by a Dundee firm. It was the first of the type to be repainted, although the doors were removed at the end of the year. Most of the rest were stored at Walnut Grove, which had become Stagecoach's new base.

Although the Edinburgh operation was sold in May 1985, Spittalfield-based A. & C. McLennan was bought in November. Eight Fleetlines included in the deal were quickly sold, but TFA 987, a Massey-bodied Daimler CCG5, was retained for two years. The bus had several claims to fame. It operated McLennan's last service, and was also the vehicle in which Brian Souter passed his PSV test. After years of neglect, it was rescued by the Burton Daimler Group, and is now kept at the town's Bass Museum.

Magicbus

During summer 1986 Stagecoach bought another five Routemasters, although one of the original batch had been dismantled for spares and one from the most recent intake was quickly sold to a private owner in Ruislip. The remainder were prepared for service at Spittalfield, although it was not yet apparent what their use would be.

In addition to the ex-London Routemasters, three former Northern General forward-entrance examples were bought. One came from the Greater London Council, another from preservationists and the third from Stevenson's of Spath. All three were prepared for use, with one retaining its Northern General livery complete with 'Shop at Binns' advertisement at the front.

The need for the additional buses became apparent on 26 October, when Stagecoach entered the Glasgow bus war, precipitated by bus deregulation. In September the Scottish Bus

Group, through its new Clydeside Scottish and Kelvin Scottish subsidiaries, had launched a major assault on Strathclyde PTE's established market, using minibuses and fleets of Routemasters. Key figures in the initiative were George Watson and Ian Manning at Clydeside and Brian Cox at Kelvin. All later went on to work for Stagecoach, and Brian Cox is now Executive Director.

For the Glasgow operation, Stagecoach established a new company called Magicbus. Three services were introduced, the principal one being the Routemaster-operated 20 linking Castlemilk with the city centre. Magicbus Routemasters — supported by Brian Souter, dressed in a 'magic bunny' outfit — were famously denied access to St Enoch Square bus station by Strathclyde Buses' inspectors on the first day. The Glasgow bus war attracted national TV coverage and Ann and Brian were interviewed, being portrayed very much as the underdogs.

Additional contract work in Glasgow employed Lodekkas, a former BEA Routemaster bought in January 1987 and the Northern General Routemasters, to which a fourth was added in March. The same month saw the arrival of another four FLFs. Three came from Cleverly of Cwmbran, but the fourth was a converted mobile caravan. Eventually painted into Stagecoach livery in 1991, it made several aid trips to Romania.

An early casualty was 847 DYE, Scotland's first Routemaster, which was withdrawn after an accident mere weeks after entering service in Glasgow.

NBC purchases

In April 1987 Stagecoach bought Hampshire Bus and Pilgrim Coaches through holding company Skipburn. The purchase brought three further Lodekkas into the fold — two FLFs and an FS. They had all been training buses, but it came as little surprise when, in August, the FS was transferred to Scotland and duly prepared for service in Stagecoach livery using seats from a withdrawn Central SMT FLF.

Seven years after it was founded, Stagecoach bought its first 'modern' double-decker buses — Van Hool-McArdle-bodied Ailsas, which were allocated to Hampshire Bus and Magicbus. It also bought a further batch of 12 Routemasters in the summer, 11 of which were initially stored at Eastleigh. Another BEA Routemaster went to Scotland, along with the 12th bus. With Southampton Citybus introducing its own fleet of Routemasters, it seemed that competition in the

city was imminent. However, events overtook what might have been planned.

In July, Skipburn took control of Cumberland Motor Services, bringing two FS6Gs into the group. One was a training bus, the other 550 (109 DRM, later AAO 547A), a 'special events' vehicle painted in a traditional Tilling-style livery. (In September 1991 it passed to the 550 Group, Workington.) But a review of Carlisle-area services led to the introduction of Routemaster operation in October 1987, mainly on service 61 between Morton Park and Harraby East via the city centre. Two buses came from the Eastleigh store, while a further six were purchased from Kelvin Scottish in August following retrenchment in Glasgow. They were painted in Cumberland's Ayres red, white and sandstone livery.

The Southampton-area operations of Hampshire Bus were sold to Musterphantom (Solent Blue Line) in October, so the balance of the Eastleigh Routemasters went north to Magicbus to operate new route 25 between St Enoch and Castlemilk via Victoria Road from November. They were joined by a further 10 buses bought direct from London Regional Transport for this and for a revised 19 route between Easterhouse and Milton, replacing Volvo coaches.

Both the 19 extension and the 25 were withdrawn after a few months following stiff competition from Strathclyde Buses. This led to some Routemasters being stored, some never to run again with Stagecoach. There were also a handful of sales. One went to the Blackburn RM Group in June 1988, while Citilink of Kingston-upon-Hull bought another, which later passed to East Yorkshire when Citilink was taken over, and worked for a while for Scarborough & District.

Two Bristol-engined FLFs were bought from a Craven Arms poultry-packer in June 1987. One was used for spares, while the other was stored before donation to Teen Challenge, a Strathclyde-area anti-alcohol/drugs campaign, in September 1989. A former Hants & Dorset FLF arrived in September 1987 from Hulme Hall, Cheadle Hulme. Although bought for spares, it was prepared for use and was the last Lodekka to enter service with Stagecoach in Scotland.

During the 1980s the company operated 34 Lodekkas. They were reliable, accessible people-movers that were cheap and easy to maintain. A wheelchair-bound passenger used to be regularly accommodated on the Perth–Spittalfield route by utilising the rear emergency door on an FLF with a ramp. This was 10 years before the Disability

Discrimination Act and long before the low-floor revolution of the mid-1990s.

A surprising arrival in August 1987, from Pencader-based Davies Bros, was DGS 625, a McLennan-bodied Leyland Tiger. Now with Bluebird Buses, this 1951 vehicle has been a high-profile member of the Stagecoach preserved fleet, attending rallies and special events, and spending several seasons in the mid-1990s on the Loch Earn 'Trundler' service to and from Crieff.

Skipburn bought a third former NBC subsidiary in November 1987. United Counties owned three Bristol FS6G trainers at the time, but half-cab operation was quickly introduced with the purchase of 16 Routemasters direct from LRT. Another four were bought in March for spares. The first eight entered service in February 1988 on Bedford cross-town service 101 between Woodside and Kempston. Corby followed in April, with the balance being used mainly on route 1, linking the town centre with the Beanfield, Welland Vale and Shire Lodge estates. Brian Souter had taken a special interest in Corby, where services had been under pressure from local taxis.

To provide cover, a Leyland-engined Routemaster was transferred from Magicbus in April and was eventually painted, like the other United Counties buses, in green with orange, yellow and cream relief. It received an AEC engine a year later. Another Magicbus Routemaster visited Bedford in December 1988 to explore the potential of a left-hand-drive conversion for a possible Japanese order.

To provide mainly mechanical spares for the Lodekka fleet in Scotland, two former Western SMT LD6Gs were bought from a building contractor in August 1988. Milton Keynes Citybus supplied another, but the last Lodekka to be secured was an FS6G, TVL 307, in April 1989. It never entered service, becoming a uniform store.

No fewer than 47 V- or W-registered Bristol VRTs had been bought by Stagecoach at the end of 1988 as part of a deal with Devon General. Three of these joined the Scottish fleet in January 1989. Others followed, signalling that the days of Lodekka operation were numbered. But perhaps the most unusual Bristol to be bought was JVW 430, a 1943 K5G, following the collapse of PK Omnibus Co in August 1988. Its purchase galvanised the preservation movement because it carried the prototype postwar ECW lowbridge body, and it passed to the Eastern National Preservation Group three months later.

Cumberland's retro-liveried Lodekka was in use as a driver trainer in 1989. The location is Whitehaven, the company's headquarters.

In the spirit

Stagecoach bought East Midland in March 1989, Ribble in April, Barrow Borough Transport's operations in May and Southdown during August, and it would be wrong to exclude from the story full-front Leyland PD3s or some of the historically-important older vehicles that have been owned by the group.

Spotting another good deal, Stagecoach had already (in August 1988) bought three of Southdown's convertible-open-top 'Queen Mary' PD3/4s via Ensignbus. Cumberland took one for intended driver training, although it hired a Blackpool Metro-Cammell-bodied PD3/11 for similar duties the following year. The other two went to United Counties as training buses.

The Ribble purchase brought several interesting vehicles into group ownership. One was a Metro-Cammell-bodied Leyland PD3/5 dating from 1963. It had been converted to a manual gearbox, and in Stagecoach ownership was regularly used for driver training. There was also a 1955 Leyland PD2/13 driver trainer. Pride of place, however, went to Ribble's pair of Leyland Lions. No 295 (CK 3825) was a 1927 PLSC1 with replica Leyland 31-seat bodywork. It was licensed as a PSV. No 296 (VY 957) was a 1929 PLSC3 with replica Roe bodywork built in 1984. Also owned, but sold to the Ribble Preservation Group in 1990, was the Lion LT5A chassis of the former Cumberland 38 (AAO 574). The two complete Lions were loaned to the Manchester Museum of Transport in the 1990s.

East Midland's purchase brought no half-cabs into the group, but new General Manager George Watson's influence was soon felt with the arrival on hire of a United Counties Routemaster at Chesterfield. It was joined by three Magicbus RMs, which were expected to be sold to Japanese corporation Nisso Iwai as part of a 30-Routemaster contract. In the event the contract fell through and they were stored. From July, Routemasters appeared in the fleet following full refurbishment and painting into a variety of striking traditional and modern liveries.

Below: **One of Speedybus's former KMB Daimler CVG6LX-34s takes a break at Foshan railway station on Boxing Day, 1996. It was one of 10 serving the city.**

Above opposite: **A Stagecoach Malawi Daimler CVG6LX-34, imported from Hong Kong.**

Below opposite: **East Midland Routemasters carried modern and traditional liveries, as seen at the Mansfield garage open day in September 1990.**

'Queen Mary' PD3/4s were involved in the deal. Two were long-term withdrawals, both being sold in 1992, while a third was the company's tree-lopper. The other two were active 'special events' vehicles, and are still owned by Stagecoach South East. Four other 'Queen Marys' were taken on as trainers. Then there was preserved 1922 Leyland G7/Short 0135 (CD 7045), transported to Perth so that it could be used by Ann Gloag for her wedding to David McCleary in July 1990, and 0813 (UF 4813), the 1929 Brush-bodied Titan TD1. More obscure was 1938 TD5 towing lorry 0184 (EUF 184).

From September 1990 route 16 between Clipstone and Mansfield was run entirely by Routemasters, but operation was short-lived. The 16 reverted to one-person operation the following June, and the last Routemaster was withdrawn in July. Three East Midland Routemasters were to have a brief reprieve during the summer of 1992 when they were used on the Sherwood Forest summer network. And one was exported to Zimbabwe, ending up at a shopping precinct in Harare.

Stagecoach acquired its next former NBC subsidiary when it purchased Southdown from its management in August 1989. Five convertible

The acquisition of Portsmouth Citybus in November 1989 added an open-top Leyland PD2/12/Metro-Cammell, along with a PD2 driver trainer, which was sold for preservation in June 1991, and a PD2/40 towing lorry. The lorry passed to Transit Holdings when Stagecoach was forced to divest its Portsmouth operation in January 1991, the open-topper following in May. It went on to operate in Oxford before moving to Torquay, only to join Stagecoach again when Transit Holdings' Devon operations were bought in January 1996. The re-acquired PD2/12 initially received Stagecoach livery, joining VRTs on open-top Torbay operation. However, for the 2000 season it was

Left: The Hastings & District-liveried Park Royal-bodied AEC Regent V on one of its rare outings on town services in October 1992.

Opposite: Busways used this Cumberland Routemaster on the Newcastle City Tour during the summer of 1996.

repainted cream and maroon in traditional Devon General 'Sea Dog' Atlantean style.

Stagecoach bought Hastings & District in December 1989. With it came a former East Kent Park Royal-bodied AEC Regent V. Within weeks work started on restoring the driver-training bus as a 'special events' PSV, and it remains in the Stagecoach South East fleet, having recently been restored to traditional East Kent maroon and cream livery.

Overseas expansion

Hong Kong-based Speedybus Enterprises was to be Stagecoach's first overseas operation. Established in November 1988, it was a 50/50 joint venture with Speedybus Services, run by Clement Lau Ming-Chuen. Time-expired Kowloon Motor Bus double-deckers had been supplied to operators in the People's Republic of China since 1986. Buses were supplied free in return for revenue generated from overall advertising, often for cigarette companies which found rich pickings in the emerging Chinese economy. However, as the project developed in the early 1990s, some Fleetlines were rented direct in Stagecoach livery before the Chinese authorities placed restrictions on certain types of advertising and the importation of further second-hand buses.

Not all the former KMB 'deckers used were Fleetlines. Long-wheelbase Daimler CVG6LX-34s with Metal Sections bodies, the newest built in 1972, were dispatched to several Chinese cities; Speedybus Services had supplied some direct, without Stagecoach involvement. All were

converted to an offside door by that company, as China drives on the right-hand side of the road. Stagecoach sold its share in Speedybus Enterprises to Mr Lau in 1993.

Perhaps the most remarkable chapter in the Stagecoach half-cab story was the supply of 60 CVG6LX-34s by Speedybus to United Transport Malawi, in which Stagecoach had acquired a 51% share during March 1989. The purchase took the company into the heart of Africa and a desperately poor country, which felt under threat from the civil war then raging along much of its southern border in neighbouring Mozambique.

Just getting the buses to Malawi was an achievement. Shipped to Durban in South Africa, hundreds of miles away, they were then driven in convoys north through that country, Zimbabwe and Zambia before reaching their final destination. Fifty-six buses entered service over a year from May 1989, mostly in Blantyre, but also in the capital city, Lilongwe. Stagecoach's reasoning for importing the buses was obvious: what became Stagecoach Malawi had limited resources, and the Daimlers' 85-seat capacity was valuable in a country where there was effectively no other form of transport.

A notable arrival in Malawi was a Bristol FLF6G which was despatched to Africa after due ceremony on 7 September 1989. There are strong cultural and religious ties between Scotland and what had been Nyasaland. Malawi's leader, Dr Hastings Banda, was a member of the Church of Scotland and had practised medicine in Scotland. Loaded with medical supplies and gifts, the bus travelled from Blantyre, Scotland, to

Southampton, where it was shipped to South Africa, eventually arriving in Blantyre, Malawi, on 3 November. Upon entering service it won praise for its improved ride quality over the Daimlers. Another FLF subsequently made a similar supply journey, arriving in May 1992, and then donated spare parts to the original bus, which by then had a failed gearbox.

The Malawian Government's decision to ban the importation of further second-hand buses precluded more half-cab arrivals, but the Daimlers gave good service, increasing loadings by nearly 60%. They were progressively replaced by high-capacity ERF Trailblazers, and the last was withdrawn in 1996. Defeated by unregulated minibus opposition, Stagecoach withdrew from the country the following year.

Not content with operating half-cabs in Asia and Africa, Stagecoach tapped a new market in late 1990, when an FLF6G was dispatched from the Scottish fleet to East Midland for an offside door conversion to be carried out. It was then shipped to Canada, joining Toronto-based Gray Coach Lines, which Stagecoach had bought in June. Numbered 1965, the year it was built, it entered service on sightseeing work and was successful enough to justify the export of a further five a year later. However, Stagecoach's Canadian adventure was not a happy one. By July 1992 Gray Coach Lines was operating under court protection, and what was left of the operation passed to Greyhound Lines of Canada on 1 January 1993.

Half-cab decline

In March 1991 Stagecoach was successful in buying its first Scottish Bus Group subsidiary — Northern Scottish Omnibuses, trading as Bluebird Northern. With it came two former Southdown Leyland PD3 driver-training buses, as well as an FLF6G tow lorry. As Bristol VRIs replaced Lodekkas in the Perth area, three FLFs were stored at Bluebird's Stonehaven garage. Later reinstated, these buses — 654-6 (GRX 129/31/2D) — were Stagecoach Scotland's last FLFs in ordinary service when withdrawn in November 1992.

August 1991 saw the demise of the United Counties Corby Routemaster operation, as Iveco minibuses were seen as the way forward in the battle with the town's taxis. Three were stored at Bedford and three more were used to bolster the 101 route allocation there.

The sale of Glasgow-based Magicbus to Kelvin Central in April 1992 drastically reduced the number of Routemasters in the Scottish operation. Five RMs were involved in the deal as well as the two BEA vehicles.

The changing face of RM980. In September 1990 RM980 was working for East Midland, painted in the company's initial post-privatisation livery. Re-registered USK 625, it had moved to Perth city services and been repainted in Stagecoach corporate colours by July 1994. In June 1998 it was working for East London after full refurbishment.

Cumberland Routemaster operation came to an end in December 1992. A moderate half-cab revival was promised when three United Counties Routemasters went to Ribble's Blackburn garage the following May for proposed operation between Manchester and Brookhouse, but nothing came of the initiative. They were stored until October 1996, when they were sold.

An initiative that did take off was the expansion of Routemaster operation in Perth. Five buses from Magicbus had been introduced to city routes in 1990. Two years later they were joined by a United Counties bus, and the three East Midland vehicles previously used on the Sherwood Forest services, although it was May 1993 before they re-entered service. Numbers were also bolstered by the re-acquisition of the two BEA buses from Kelvin Scottish in August 1993, following the end of that operator's Routemaster operation in July.

United Counties Routemaster operation in Bedford ended in September 1993, Stagecoach having invested in new Alexander-bodied Volvo B6s, which also replaced Leyland Nationals and Bristol VRTs in the town.

But not the end

As Stagecoach grew in the 1990s, penny numbers of half-cabs came and went. Its purchase of Newcastle-based Busways on 26 July 1994 brought three East Lancs-bodied PD3 trainers into the group, but within months they were up for sale. Busways also had a highly regarded collection of historic vehicles, which included an ex-South Shields Roe-bodied Daimler CCG6 as a 'special events' vehicle, and a former Newcastle all-Leyland PD2/1. The Titan went to the Northern Counties Bus Preservation Group, but the Daimler remained with Busways.

Western Scottish, bought by the group in August 1994, also owned preserved buses — a rare 1963 Alexander-bodied Albion Lowlander LR3 and Titan PD3A/3 which remain in stock with what is now Western Buses. Cleveland Transit was secured the following December, and this yielded another convertible Southdown 'Queen Mary'. It has since earned its keep on a variety of

work, spending the summers of 1999 and 2000 on a shoppers' service in Hartlepool.

Chesterfield Transport, bought in 1995 and absorbed into East Midland the following year, was instrumental in the return of a 1960 Weymann-bodied PD2/30 which had been preserved by the undertaking, only to be dispatched in September 1986 to HEAG Transport of Darmstadt, Germany. The bus was placed in the care of Chesterfield Borough Council on its return to the UK.

The acquisition of Cambus Holdings in December 1995 brought with it two Lodekkas. A Viscount Bus & Coach FLF6G in Peterborough & District livery had seen regular service on the town's routes and had made regular rally appearances, while Premier Travel's open-top FLF had also had a high profile. In 1999 and 2000 both buses were used on summer routes 60/61 linking Peterborough, Ferry Meadows and Sacrewell. The open-topper was repainted in Stagecoach livery for the service.

Legislation had forced most remaining half-cabs off driver training work in the early 1990s, but Greater Manchester Buses (South) still owned a 1964 Massey-bodied ex-Wigan PD2A/27 when the company joined the group in March 1996. It lasted a year before being sold.

What had become Bluebird Buses' Routemaster operation in Perth came to an end in December 1996, when nine Alexander ALX200-bodied Volvo B6LEs replaced them on the 1/2 City Centre–Letham–Tulloch circular. Seven buses went into

Below: **The ultimate half-cab in the ultimate setting? East London's RML2760 at Marble Arch in London in August 1995.**

Left: **This Leyland Tiger PS1/2 with McLennan coachwork has been a good ambassador for Stagecoach. Here it is at the Scottish Vintage Bus Museum in September 1996, complete with Loch Earn Trundler logo.**

Inset opposite: **As seen here, Stagecoach Devon's Leyland Titan PD2/12 was initially painted in corporate livery, although in 2000 it was repainted in Devon General cream and dark red. The bus was new to Portsmouth Corporation.**

storage at Western Buses' Cumnock garage, although one was off the road for only a short period. To mark the absorption by Western Buses of the A1 Service business, bought in 1995, it was painted in A1 blue and cream livery. Like other members of Stagecoach's preserved Scottish fleet, it can often be found at the Scottish Vintage Bus Museum. The A1 services were merged into Western's operation in July 1997.

Rather than sell its stock of Cumberland and United Counties Routemasters, Stagecoach decided to establish a strategic reserve that could be used as a competitive tool if the need arose. Fifteen buses were involved, and all were repainted into Stagecoach livery early in 1994. In the event, there was no mass return to service, although buses were occasionally re-licensed for special events and rallies. Perhaps the longest re-licensing was of a Cumberland bus during summer 1996, when it worked the Newcastle City Tour along side an open-top Atlantean. Busways allocated it to the Blue Bus Services subsidiary, giving it appropriate fleetnames.

Most of the reserve Routemasters were sold to PVS, Carlton, in 1999, but, following London Buses' decision to re-establish a strategic reserve following the creation of Transport for London, three moved back to the capital.

London's unique market conditions have given Routemasters an extended life way beyond what was envisaged when the bus was originally

designed. Their manœuvrability and speed of operation are still valued, and they have become a tourist attraction in their own right. Privatisation of London Buses in the mid-1990s saw Stagecoach buy two subsidiaries, Selkent and East London, which joined the group in September 1994. Selkent owned just two half-cabs — former Green Line coaches RMC1490 and RMC1515, the latter converted to open-top. Both were stored with Cumberland, but RMC1490 quickly moved to Perth, where it was used in December as a mobile hoarding for the park-and-ride service operated from St Johnstone football ground. It later joined the Stagecoach preserved fleet.

The purchase of East London brought 61 Routemasters into Stagecoach ownership, and their continued operation represents the last bastion of regular half-cab working by the company. The 54 long RML types included historically important RML2760, the last Routemaster built, which retained an AEC engine; the rest had Iveco units. Of two standard Routemasters, RM613 was in 'showbus' condition, while RM1527 was regularly used in the *EastEnders* TV soap opera. Two former BEA coaches had also been returned to PSV use and were regularly used in service, as were three former Green Line RMC-class coaches.

Under Stagecoach ownership the East London Routemasters were repainted with cream bands and gold underlined fleetnames, which suited them well. RMC1461, however, caused a sensation when it was repainted in full Green Line livery, which it still retains; RMC1485 appeared in a red-based version of the Green Line livery in 1997. Following trials in 1998 with Cummins-engined RML2451, and RML2665 with a Scania engine, the balance of the East London RML fleet was re-engined with Scania units, although this did not include RML2760.

Notable transfers were the departure of the two BEA coaches to Stagecoach Portugal in February 1998, their place being taken by three of the Bluebird Routemasters stored at Cumnock. Before being shipped to Portugal the BEA Routemasters were converted to offside-centre-door and open-top. The Portuguese business had been established in 1995 when Rodoviaria de Lisboa was purchased by Stagecoach jointly with Montagu Private Equity.

The Portuguese buses are not Stagecoach's only overseas Routemasters. The purchase of Hong Kong Citybus in March 1999 brought with it two much-rebuilt 'special events' buses which had been RM1288 and RM1873 with London Transport. Ironically it was their export in 1984 and subsequent demonstration in China which paved the way for Speedybus's activities a few years later.

Stagecoach Chairman Brian Souter is a man of firm views, and this has sometimes made him a controversial figure. Yet it is these strong personal convictions which have focused the business and led to such widespread use of half-cab buses by the group. And rumour has it that Doncaster minibus converter Crest converted a Routemaster into a mobile caravan for the Souter family in 2000. So if you see one off the beaten track, have a careful look at the driver. You might get a surprise!

Below: **Two United Counties Routemasters at Bedford in April 1989. The bus on the left, re-registered in Scotland, had previously worked for Magicbus.**

THE ISLAND'S *EIGHTH* *WONDER?*

You are hurtling along at vast (or relatively vast) speed, lurching wildly round corners, plunging violently down a short but very sharp gradient to a chorus of 'Ooohs!' and immediately up a short but very sharp gradient to a chorus of 'Aaahs!' and then screeching to a shuddering stop, hurled forward in your seat. All this isn't a grossly over-priced helter-skelter ride at a theme park; the chorus of 'Ooohs!' and 'Aaahs!' comes merely from a pack of OAPs or senior citizens on the upper deck of a regular service bus (admittedly at pretty exorbitant fares) running behind-time with an out-of-temper driver on route 7 or 7A of Southern Vectis along the narrow, sinuous and prone-to-landslip vicissitudes of the Undercliff road to Ventnor on the Isle of Wight and being brought to a sudden halt by the twelfth motor coach coming the other way in less than 12 minutes.

Now this thrilling and delightful mode of progress may be caught but a minute's walk from my front door. Regular readers of *Buses Yearbook* (those who don't skip the Jowitt pages on the grounds of their being too much about girls and not enough about buses) may possibly recall that for the past 10 years Jowitt and family have resided in Herefordshire; but for the sake of a warmer climate and proximity to the sea and

An exploration by bus of the Isle of Wight, famous for seven unlikely wonders, in the usual discerning and discursive style of Robert E. Jowitt, who thinks he may have found an eighth to add to the list.

View from Jowitt's bathroom window, on 2 February 2000, of a Volvo Olympian/ Northern Counties on the 7 which left Ryde at 11.15 and is passing the White Lion at Niton at 12.39. Despite its tourist proclivities, the Island boasts some shocking wire-scapes...
All photographs by the author

types as the Hants & Dorset buses I could see any day at home in Winchester.

Of the Isle of Wight coaches, however, in the late 1950s, I did have some experience. My father would certainly never have considered a vulgar Round-the-Island tour — though at that date there were many on offer from several operators — but, as Secretary of the Hampshire Field Club & Archæological Society, he organised an annual exploration of the Isle of Wight for the members to study geology and archæology, and these parties were conveyed to the sites of geological or archæological interest in Shotters' Bedford OBs or similar antiques.

Then, in the mid-1960s, when the remainder of the Island's steam railways were under threat of wiping-out, I did an intensive steam-grice and hated the buses right heartily. Later again, with my mother and father still being requested to write Isle of Wight guide books — the demand appears insatiable for everything from discerning essays (such as my parents' work and this piece) to absolute arrant nonsense — I was called upon to take photos of notable Island scenes, into which, with demise of steam a *fait accompli*, I condescended to slip a bus or two. A Lodekka and perhaps even a VR or a Leyland National were just about worth including.

Then, when with young family far from sea in Herefordshire and an annual holiday to a friend's IoW holiday cottage a vital feature of life, the now almost all-Leyland and then Volvo fleet became more alluring.

Leaving the bottom corner of my garden in Niton, the bus is soon descending to the Undercliff. This is an interesting tract of land some five miles long and seldom more than a few hundred yards wide, caused by the cliff falling down in prehistoric times and creating a rumpled shelf sloping down to the sea. Before proceeding eastwards along this, the bus first performs a clockwise loop of nearly half a mile through some incredibly narrow twisting lanes to serve a few

numerous other reasons far too lengthy to set down here Jowitt and family removed to the Isle of Wight, which — and this is a reason which *must* be set down — enjoys a far more intensive (though unfortunately far more expensive) bus service than anything rural Herefordshire can offer.

Even as I write these words, sitting on a garden bench (*ex* top deck of Bournemouth tram) in the sun, I can see the roof of a Vectis Leyland Olympian coasting past beyond my somewhat unkempt hedge, and I know that in an hour I shall, if still sitting here, see another. And so on…

I suppose I have known Southern Vectis for more than half a century. I have certainly known the Isle of Wight that long, for my little sister and I were brought by our parents for two holidays at Seaview while the parents were writing a guidebook on the Island for Batsford. I remember annoying my mother very much by weeping all the way home for distress at leaving the Island. Perhaps that is why, 50 years later, I have come back. But I have returned here before, and often…

On those first two holidays we travelled about the Island in the family Vauxhall and had nothing to do with public transport save for a ride on a mechanical elephant in Ryde. Then in the early 1950s, when the Island's railways were under threat, my father brought me over on day trips with day-tickets to explore these rural branches and to study incidentally how hopelessly inadequate the buses would be at coping with the number of huge ornate perambulators then in vogue and which could be carried so easily in the elderly ex-LBSCR or LSWR guards' vans. The buses were of no interest anyway because, at least to my untutored eye, they were the same colour and the same houses (whose owners probably seldom use the bus but often park their cars in its way) and the famous Buddle Inn, mentioned in tourist brochures as a haunt of smugglers.

In the case of inns and taverns advertised in the brochures, I will say, while not being specific and not having sampled all of them, that in my experience the larger the advertisement the more you are likely to be served by truculently arrogant crop-headed youths who despise you and then have your food brought to you a very long time after you ordered it by amiable but dim female students, only to discover that it isn't what you ordered. Not that it makes any difference, for one army canteen dish tastes much like another. There are plenty of excellent pubs which don't advertise at all.

To return to the bus, note here that the westbound buses serve the same loop in the same direction, so in summer you can see three buses an hour here. This is the most southerly point of the Isle of Wight — thus obviously the furthest south served by Southern Vectis — and you can see St Catherine's Lighthouse, which marks the bottom point of the Island diamond map, from the windows of the bus; if you happen to be looking in the right direction.

We now proceed eastbound along the Undercliff, in the fashion described in the first paragraph. Given the nature of the terrain, the road is narrow and twisty, and, given its scenic splendour, it is the delight of coach tour operators; these, by its limitations, are permitted only to use it westwards, but they make the most of this privilege and strongly resent in various Welsh and Scottish and Midlands accents the eastbound passage of indigenous stage-carriage buses at every head-on meeting.

Our bus brings us lurchingly over bends and gradients into the town of Ventnor, with its streets

Above: **In the high summer of 1997 we see Dennis Dart 813, new the previous year, picking up a healthy load of tourists in the high Victorian splendours of Ventnor.**

Opposite: **Sisters 687 and 688 of the 1982 Leyland Olympian/ECW delivery are here at rest in Ventnor depot with a Ventnor mini-skirt lingering on the pavement outside... but aren't trainers a fashion disaster area?**

and terraces of choice 19th-century villas spread in a series of ledges down — or up — the cascading undulations of the Undercliff, in fashion compared favourably, as is its climate, with resorts such as Menton or Monte Carlo in ancient guide books. Even today the *Sunday Times* gives it a plug now and then. It has a slightly sordid aura of dereliction and boarded-up shops unable to cope with the competition from the Costa Brava mingled with a rather charming sense of decadent decay. Also it can claim what I believe to be the miniest mini-skirt I have ever beheld in all my years of bus photography.

Ventnor is the meeting-place of several bus routes. Attentive readers will have noted I have come hither from Niton on a 7 or 7A, but I could equally have come on a 6, which for a mile or so passes along the top of the aforementioned cliffs with a fairly frightening view over their edge to the Undercliff and the beach far below; or on a 31, the local midibus which provides a service of such complex meanderings that neither the locals nor even an experienced traveller and timetable student such as myself can understand them.

On departing from Ventnor to continue the journey there are various options, namely 6, 7, 7A, 92 and 93. In dealing with the first last, I will say that all the rest ascend (this ascent including a piece of what looks like 1-in-5 landslip) to a district known as Upper Ventnor, then to the flourishing but

unattractive village of Wroxall and a roundabout with bungalows known as Whitely Bank, whence 7 and 7A head east for Shanklin and 92 and 93 west for Newport. The 92 until recent times carried on from Newport to West Cowes to meet the arrivals and departures of Red Jet ferries to Southampton and was operated by 1996 Dennis Darts with 'Jetlink' logo. This facility has now been withdrawn, presumably because of the impossibility of keeping to the timetable, and, much to the fury of the inhabitants of Ventnor, you have to change in Newport; the logos have been — more or less — removed from the Darts.

I must relate how I once had occasion to travel on the 92 on one of the two remaining 1980 Bristol LH buses, with one driver (not unreasonably) driving and another sitting immediately behind him. The (first) driver lost his gears on the hairpin bend just above Ventnor Trinity Church — which requires even the best of drivers to pull over onto the wrong side of the road when ascending — and started to roll back. This problem resolved, he managed the rest of the ascent from Ventnor with only minor mishap but then, coming down into Wroxall, he

Village, with its abundance of thatched-roofed and barge-boarded taverns and gifte shoppes (selling souvenirs such as Edwardian-clad dolls, plaster pirates and mermaids and traditional glass devices filled with the famous coloured sands of Alum Bay) and a frightful double S-bend amidst them which must be an awful trial to any bus or coach driver.

The rest of Shanklin is mostly mundane, if not devoid of Victorian architectural gems, most of them converted to hotels... or perhaps even built as such in the first place. Into their narrow driveways the coach drivers on IoW tours thrust enormous vehicles with consummate skill onto spots where you wouldn't think you could fit even a Ford Fiesta.

Shanklin's chief claim to bus fame was, a few years ago, an RELL converted to topless form and known as 'Shanklin's Pony', featuring as such on the summer 1988 Southern Vectis timetable, and operating a 20-minute service on route 44 between the town and the esplanade. I deeply regret to say I never managed to photograph this bus, but I regret even more that I was not present at an occasion related to me by a lady visitor to Shanklin on which a number of ingenuous female foreign students, arriving on the beach, assumed their innocent native habit of disporting themselves topless — like the bus — before being warned off by some local prude. What a foreground would this have provided for photos of 'Shanklin's Pony'!

At this date Shanklin was served also by open-top double-deckers, probably VRs, on a route numbered 45 coming through from the Tropical Bird Gardens west of Ventnor and following what is now the 6 (then the 16 or 16A — there have been drastic renumberings over the years) to Shanklin and on to Sandown. The 45 has long since faded away, and the Tropical Birds have flown. The 44, however, has replaced the 45 between Shanklin and Sandown, passing in the mid-1990s through a stage of being entitled The Big Dipper, with open-top VRs painted in lurid livery of purple and pale green squares, and most recently described as 'The Village Bus' in what purports to be original SV colours, which look just like old Southdown.

If we don't elect to travel on to Sandown by the 44 we may take the 6 or 7 or 7A thither, through continuous conurbation, variously Victorian and bungaloid, via a place called Lake. The village of Lake can claim no guide book merits save only inasmuch as it is one of the seven wonders of the Isle of Wight. It must here be explained to those readers unfamiliar with Island postcards and tea-towels that the seven wonders of the Isle of Wight

took the tortuous descent in top gear at high speed. Fortunately no one was waiting at the stop halfway down the grade, and at the next stop on the next hill-top the other driver took over...

This is perhaps the moment to add that the 7 and 7A, even while they go inland from Ventnor, are known as the Island Explorer, in special blue livery with lurid stick-ons of notable Island attractions, such services being intended to replace the now vanished round-the-Island efforts of erstwhile private operators. These vehicles include two of the 1993 Leyland Olympian/Northern Counties and five 1998 Volvo Olympians.

To pursue the course round the perimeter of the Island from Ventnor, it is necessary, however, to catch a 6, which, after the Trinity zig-zag and a dramatic ascent on a ledge to the upper heights of the villa-dotted eastern extremity of Ventnor or the popular Victorian resort of Bonchurch, follows voluptuous curves along the bosom of the seaward-descending downs with far-reaching views of Culver Cliff (the eastern end of the Island) and the coast of Sussex extending into the distance (on a fine day) before descending to Shanklin Olde

are in fact of a negative nature, and Lake is a typical example, 'the lake which has no water'. The place possesses not even a pond.

Another alternative is the 23. This is operated by Wightbus, a council-owned concern which, while dealing mainly in schools transport, also attends to the routes which SV doesn't, with a motley fleet including wheelchair-lift midibuses, long-wheelbase Dennis Darts, and (at the time of writing, though probably not of reading) the Island's longest and highest and largest double-decker, a Leyland Olympian/ECW 72-seater coach which came to Wightbus in 1993 from Cumbria via a dealer,

having been new in 1983 to London Country — a deal Wightbus subsequently tended to regret. This monster comes regularly to Shanklin on schools, but never works on the 23, for the route follows many very narrow and tree-bedecked lanes. It is the slowest and most round-about possible way of travelling from Shanklin to Sandown but does afford an interesting view of the resorts' hinterland, with some not unattractive old villages and the rumply hills of the Lower Greensand.

Sandown is magnificently vulgar, with miles of golden sand and a mixture of choice Victorian architecture and subsequent dreadfulness and any number of shops devoted to selling Edwardian-clad dollies, plaster pirates and mermaids, and traditional glass devices filled with coloured sands...

From Sandown, if we wish to proceed as far as is possible round the perimeter of the Island by bus, we must abandon the 6 or 7 or 7A in favour of the 1. The former routes cut straight across the eastern triangle of the Island to Ryde via Brading, which is famous for its bull-ring (a rusty circle of metal enshrined in the paving stones), its doll museum (worth a visit, as the guide books state),

Opposite: **View from St Boniface Down, highest point on the Island, to show how buses on 6 and 7, leaving the route through Ventnor's Victoriana behind, have to swing onto the wrong side of the road at Trinity Church to face the zig-zag which, palm-tree-clad, marks the division of routes via Wroxall or Upper Bonchurch.**

Below: **Back in a golden age, little perhaps as Jowitt then appreciated it, on 27 June 1977 Ryde Esplanade was background to Lodekkas and VRs. The 'poppy green' (if so we can describe it) was probably a bit of a put-off.**

its waxworks (which I have never visited but which have been described to me as having a tacky and outdated charm) and its Roman villa pavements (mentioned by my parents in their 1950 guide book as being protected by a tin shed of repellent appearance — which now, half a century later, is in danger of imminent collapse).

The serious seeker for round-Island bus travel will, however, avoid Brading by catching a 1. This goes as far east — almost — as it is possible to go in the Island, though the easternmost extremity of the bus route is a housing estate which might be anywhere. This is in the village of Bembridge, from where the bus continues over an embankment with shore decorated by fascinatingly varied styles of houseboat. This bank prevents the sea from spreading, as in days of yore it did, to Brading and nearly to Sandown. Back to land at St Helens, a mild village spread around a green, and on to Nettlestone, with a string of semi-detached villas in fanciful Vic Goth, all named after famous public schools. Here we catch a number 8, for while the 1 continues inland to Ryde the 8 hugs the shore at Seaview. Service 8 has enjoyed or endured many changes of bus in the last decade, its most exciting phase

being 'Big Dipper' chequered open-top VRs which provided an exhilarating ride round the many right-angle bends between Seaview and Nettlestone. It now enjoys or endures a mixture of Darts, Iveco midibuses and perhaps an occasional LHS.

Ryde is another wonder of the Isle of Wight. 'Ryde where you walk!' Oh dear!

Ryde is one of the principal entries to the Island for mainlanders. Its lengthy pier, served by the railway — formerly steam and now vintage London Underground electric — and also until 35 years ago by a tram variously in the course of its life powered by horse and petrol and diesel, is described in elderly editions of the Ward-Lock 'Red Guide' as 'looking like a centipede'; the crowds of

The Isle of Wight girl-in-the-street in all her glory, twiddling the heart round her neck on her forefinger, though it must be said again that trainers are far from elegant footwear. If the emerald or turquoise livery of the buses in this 1992 shot is long since dead, it is still possible — though who can say for how much longer? — to see a Bristol VR flanked by Leyland Olympians on Ryde Esplanade.

holidaymakers who came in their hundreds on paddle-steamers are now replaced by crowds in tens on catamarans.

From the end of July until the beginning of September Ryde thrives gaudily as a holiday resort; the rest of the time it is a rather sad place, with a plainly poverty-stricken population and as many charity shops as any other shops, apart from boarded-up shops. Fond as I am of the place I cannot bear it, for it is filled for me with romantic and emotional promises of a future which proved to be unfulfilled, so I am only too glad to catch the next bus out.

The Island Explorer or 7/7A from here makes no attempt to follow the coast, but goes inland via Havenstreet, with its station on the famous Isle of Wight Steam Railway.

The Osborne Estate is perhaps one of the reasons why no buses follow the coast from Ryde westwards. The best we can manage on this score is a number 4, usually a midibus, through Binstead and Wootton along what was, according to my father, the second-most dismal stretch of road on the Island, even if redeemed with a rather charming glimpse of Wootton Creek with its mud and houseboats; then, following the perimeters of the estate past lodges which, when house agents are trying to sell them, they will describe as being designed by Albert the Prince Consort, we arrive in East Cowes.

East Cowes is the arrival point of the famous Red Funnel car ferry, and motorists thus arrived speed through it and out of it as fast as they can; I don't say I blame them, though here, as the tortuous and tedious bus ride proves, there is an architectural wealth well worth studying.

East Cowes is on the opposite side of the River Medina from West Cowes, and the two are linked by a chain ferry. At one stage, a decade or so ago, SV operated a midibus which used this ferry. This route was, however, abandoned, so now, if you wish to travel by bus from East Cowes to West Cowes, you have to go via Newport.

Newport is another of those negative seven wonders of the Island: 'New Port which you cannot bottle!' Oh, ha ha ha! It is also the administrative capital of the Isle of Wight, and is basically an old-fashioned market town with a delightful harbour on the Medina (swans, yachts and even small cargo boats) and a very un-delightful fringe of light industries. The streets of Newport abound in the typical Isle of Wight girl, generally a big-boned but far from uncomely creature, if not without a degree of Edinburgh-like hardness in her cast of countenance, usually these days clad in black trousers tight down to the knees and flared below and, in summer, a crop top revealing a ring in her navel. The streets also abound in SV buses, for from the bus station routes radiate like the transversals of a spider's web in half a dozen directions to every part of the Island.

There are very frequent buses from Newport to West Cowes, past the gloomy walls of Parkhurst and associated prisons. West Cowes is far more prominent in the social calendar than East Cowes, as it is the scene of Cowes Week and the home of the yacht squadron associated therewith, and of no possible appeal to those persons interested in buses save that during Cowes Week a special quasi-park-and-ride system is operated by Wightbus to solve otherwise impossible traffic problems. Either East Cowes or West Cowes or possibly collectively the two Cowes provide another of the wonders of the Isle of Wight, being 'the cows you cannot milk!'

West Cowes spreads out in terraced Victorian splendour over several hills and intervening valleys comparable to (if less dramatic than) the seven

The Island's largest double-decker (see text for details), with foreground of municipal flora and a Parisian-style lamp and a background of the 'centipede' of Ryde Pier.

hills of Lisbon, and the SV buses pursue incomprehensible courses through this terrain in a series of right-angles and steep grades not unlike the Lisbon trams. The outer fringes of Cowes, consisting of modernity and light industry, are less alluring.

If we would continue our journey along the outermost extremities of IoW bus routes — along the northwest coast — we would need to dabble with the 33 and 35, but these are midibus routes serving a district which, if not devoid of rural charm, certainly lacks the dramatic and scenic appeal of other parts of the Island. Furthermore, this journey would bring us to a dead end in Newtown, from which we would have to retrace our route to West Cowes.

From West Cowes, therefore, let us return to Newport. From here, on one or another of the spines of the spider's web, we could go on a 2 or 92 to Godshill — highly rated in guide books and boasting a model village of Godshill with a model village in the model village (and *reductio ad absurdum*) but otherwise less attractive than several other Island villages — or on a 6 via bold downland scenery to Niton where we started, or on a 12 via more bold downland scenery to Shorwell and Brook where we would join the 7 and 7A; but what we will actually do is catch the 7 or 7A radial of the web west from Newport.

It is this part of the route which accounts for the fact of there being a 7 and a 7A. All round the other three-quarters of the Island they are exactly the same route, but between Newport and

Yarmouth the 7 travels among wind-bent oaks along the flat agricultural lands of the north west, passing at Shalfleet (notable church tower) within a mile of that dead-end midibus route to Newtown, while the 7A, a mile or so to the south, follows the northern flank of the central backbone ridge of the Island, with glimpses of the Solent looking like a lake and, if you are lucky, glimpses of the celebrated red squirrels leaping from branch to branch over the roof of the bus.

The 7 and 7A join together again just before Yarmouth. Yarmouth is the arrival port for the ferry from Lymington and boasts a renowned yacht harbour. From here the 7 and 7A are joined by the 42, usually worked by open-top Lodekkas, proceeding via the fading Victorian opulence of Colwell and Totland to Alum Bay. This is where the famous coloured sands are to be found, the result of geological upheaval. Passing over a huge coach park and a chair lift and several other modern attractions, we can continue on the Lodekka, with a splendid retrospective view of the twisted strata of the coloured sands, along an absolutely terrifying road above a steep cliff to the Needles — three chalk blocks sticking up out of the sea and marking the westward end of the Island. These represent another of the Island's wonders, being 'needles you cannot thread!'

At the time of writing Bristols still survive — a handful of VRs and a delightful pair of ECW-bodied LHS6Ls, the latter seen here with a background of Newport Victorian terraces and thundery clouds in March 1999.

Returning heart-in-mouth along this awesome edge we can change at Alum Bay onto the 7 or 7A or 12 and, after the delightful if decaying villas of Totland, turn right through Freshwater. This village is yet another Island wonder, being 'fresh water which you can't drink!' South of Freshwater is Freshwater Bay, at one time famous for having an arched rock of chalk; this collapsed in a gale some years since, and the Council considered rebuilding it, but wiser counsels prevailed. In Freshwater Bay the stops in both directions are immediately opposite each other, and when SV buses stop thus and their drivers indulge in conversation the holiday motorist traffic is held up for many minutes.

Beyond here the 7, 7A and 12 carry on over the top of a most alarming chalk cliff with a sheer drop to the sea and wind gauges and sundry memorials to persons who failed to stay on the road. We now descend to Compton Bay, noted for dinosaur footprints. The road hereabouts is liable to descend at any moment in a landslip to the beach, which would be of some inconvenience to the 7, 7A and 12. The next halt is Brook, a scattered hamlet with some claim to being one of the wonders of the Island inasmuch as there is no stream there so you can't wet your feet in it. From Brook the 12 turns inland, to follow the southern flank of the central ridge through Mottistone to Shorwell before turning north to Newport, while the 7 and 7A carry on along what is known as the Military Road, this being one of those Victorian preventive measures against proposed French invasions which never happened.

Except for a few holiday camps of Auschwitz appearance, the Military Road is devoid of population and, except for a couple of zig-zag bends for no apparent reason in flat fields, it affords a fine high-speed run. Dangerous paths lead down gullies or chines to miles of empty beaches where formality in bathing attire is not *de rigueur*. From the top deck of the 7 — or the 7A — you can see the 12 hacking along below the downs, and you can see back to Freshwater and the white cliffs leading ferociously to the Needles, and you can see ahead to the great summit of St Catherine's.

Apart from VRs, the oldest double-decker in the Southern Vectis fleet is Leyland Olympian/ECW 686, of 1982 vintage, here surrounded in Newport bus station in 2000 by three all-Leyland Olympians of 1989. Note that all four are carrying front advertisements for *The Merry Widow*, for which production the scenery was designed by Robert Jowitt. Frontal adverts are somewhat of a rarity on the Island.

Above: **From Newport, bus routes radiate through the manifold charms of Island scenery. What we see here is a large section of the 6A, with Newport just beyond the horizon and Niton a mile behind the camera. The bus is actually on service 6 diverted by roadworks, and has all-over adverts for the County Press, the Island's local paper.**

At this point it is worth considering a trip on Wightbus route 36, once a day in each direction, which wanders erratically via every point of the compass and off-the-beaten-track lanes through the primitively rural countryside contained between the 12, the 7 and the 6. To obtain full value from this you need to sample the morning run, because, if no one boards the bus in some of its wilder deviations on the inward trip to Newport, the wilder deviations are excluded by the driver on the return working.

Meanwhile, back on the 7 — or 7A — after the bleak village of Chale, where the 6, coming from Newport, joins us, we start to ascend to the saintly high hill, calling *en route* at Blackgang Chine, one of the Island's most famous tourist traps, which, even in the early years of the 20th century, boasted the skeleton of a whale in the middle of its bazaar and now adds dinosaurs and a maze and almost anything else you can imagine, and is thus an important timing point for SV services during the tourist season. It serves as such in winter, too, even when it is closed and empty, so the buses proceed to its abandoned portals for no apparent

purpose. The buses then grind upwards, with a view rearwards on clear days to Portland, 50 miles distant, to the highest point reached by Southern Vectis buses, some 530ft above sea level, not far below the mediæval lighthouse known as the Pepperpot, which, at 780ft, is the second-highest point on the Island (only 10ft lower than St Boniface Down, above Ventnor). When the Atlantic gales are howling across St Catherine's it is well-nigh impossible to hold a double-decker to its straight and narrow course, and I have sampled some pretty exciting sessions of hither and thither over these heights, before descending to the tranquillity of Niton. Which was where we first started this journey…

It must be obvious from the above that Southern Vectis offers an excellent service over a remarkable variety of scenic and architectural delights. Against this I can offer only two complaints. One is that, since I started writing these words, SV has decided on a re-vamp of its services, so that some (at least) of the routes described herein, notably from Sandown to Bembridge, will probably be no more than history by the time these words appear on the printed page, while at the same time several of the older Leylands have had their traditional DL Isle of Wight registration plates replaced by senseless Irish TIL numbers… Is this to hide the age of the bus?

The other and much more serious complaint, and one voiced by many Island residents, is the question of fares. The Jowitt family, consisting of husband, wife, teenage daughter, two half-fare sons and one under-age son, considered taking monthly tickets for travelling together round the Island by bus for August 2000. This would have worked out at £210. The basic cost of keeping the nearly derelict family banger going for a year is £300, to which add petrol and sundry repairs, but…

The eighth wonder of the Isle of Wight is surely that the inhabitants, unless perforce they have no other alternative, simply cannot afford the bus fares. But then, as I said near the start, the wonders of the Isle of Wight are mostly in the negative.

And, even if you can't afford it, SV is still by far the best way of travelling round the Island…

At the start of 2001 Southern Vectis introduced wide-ranging changes to its routes, with the most visible being the introduction of 'Route Rouge' branding on a fleet of red-liveried Olympians allocated to the 2, 3, 3A and 3B running from Cowes to Sandown, Shanklin and Ventnor.

Below left: **Meanwhile, down at Yarmouth in National Bus Company days, we have a Lodekka heading for Alum Bay while VRs pursue their round-Island routes. Today we could still see a Lodekka, though not in that livery; the others would be Volvos.**

Below: **Right on the target, a 1998 Volvo Olympian/Northern Counties pauses a moment at Blackgang Chine. The Island Explorer livery of these buses, dedicated to round-the-Island services, has now been altered to accommodate incongruous upper-deck advertisements.**

OVER THE SEA
TO SKYE

Roy Marshall looks back at buses on Skye, the Scottish island shrouded in romance — and, more often, rain.

In 1954 my father and I purchased our first car with the object of having both touring holidays and weekend days out, now that we enjoyed additional holiday leave and free Saturdays.

Our first touring holiday was to the west coast of Scotland and the islands, including the Isle of Skye. *En route* we came across a policeman on point duty at Sheil Bridge who remonstrated with me for failing to signal my intended turn. He apologised when I pointed out that I had signalled with the car's flashing indicators — these were the first he had ever seen!

Skye was reached via Kyle of Lochalsh and the frequent shuttle ferry to Kyleakin. Kyle is the rail terminus for services from Inverness, while a rail line from Fort William terminates at Mallaig. Here a second ferry operated to Armadale on Skye. In 1954 MacBrayne's ran the bus service between Armadale and Kyleakin, having acquired the business of MacLean & MacDonald in 1948. This was one of several island services which also carried the Royal Mail in a locked rear compartment on the bus.

The trunk service between Kyleakin, Broadford and Portree was one of those operated by Skye Transport, owned by the Scottish Co-operative Wholesale Society which had bought it from D. J. Nicolson of Portree in 1948. He had pioneered the service in the 1920s, had sold it to Highland Transport in March 1930 and then bought it back again in 1935 after Highland Transport had suffered three years of financial losses. Neil Beaton of Portree had been another important operator, but had pulled out of local bus operation in the early 1950s, various smaller operators taking over the services.

At this time most roads were in need of repair, were narrow with passing places, and had restrictions on vehicle weights and dimensions. Sunday continued to be observed as the day of rest; no ferries or bus services ran apart from those for churchgoers. No petrol stations or shops opened, accommodation signs were covered, and Sunday milk deliveries were made on Saturday evenings. However, Sunday newspapers mysteriously appeared...

Tourism was becoming more popular, but, despite the jobs this created, many of the younger generation were leaving in pursuit of better prospects on the mainland. The Cuillins, popular with hikers and rock climbers, had been a regular attraction for several years. These mountains attract cloud and give Skye the name 'Isle of Mist'.

At that time the island was also served by a boat which called at Mallaig, Kyle of Lochalsh, Portree and thence across to Stornoway on the Isle of Lewis. Any vehicles were loaded by sling. Many visitors arrived by rail, which fed them to the boat and, via the ferry, to the buses.

In subsequent years the growth of road traffic led to road improvements both on the mainland and the island, resulting in the withdrawal of the boat service and its replacement by a roll-on/roll-off ferry between Uig (Skye) and Tarbert (Harris), whilst more recently a toll bridge has replaced the ferry at Kyle.

Crofting and fishing were interesting to observe, but both activities are now considerably reduced. The beauty of the island, however, has drawn me back several times.

Opposite above: **The Marshall family Ford, on its first touring holiday to Skye in August 1954, encounters a Bedford OWB near Uig. It has an SMT body and was operated by MacLeod of Duntulm on a route linking Kilmalaig and Portree. It had been new to Alexander.**

Opposite below: **This neat little Bedford was operated by MacKinnon of Elgol on a service to Broadford. In 1972 the route was converted to Postbus operation.**

Right: **MacBrayne's was for many years a major presence on Skye, where its fleet included this neat Thornycroft with bodywork by Croft of Glasgow. It was new in 1950 and is seen in Portree in 1954.**

Below right: **The use of this style of Austin K-series chassis, with its new-look bonnet, as the basis of a bus was relatively rare, in Britain at any rate. This one was operated by Macrae of Carbost and is seen at Sligachan's Inn, collecting passengers from Skye Transport's Kyleakin to Portree service. The Austin is bound for Carbost, Portnalong and Fiskavaig.**

Below: **A Skye Transport Albion AZ9N with SCWS body heads south near Sconser on its way to Broadford and Kyleakin.**

Above: An older and more conventional Austin operated by Nicolson of Skeabost Bridge, seen in Portree in 1960. The service was taken over by Carson of Dunvegan in 1965.

Right: MacPhie of Shaggary was another Austin operator, running a service from Portree to Dunvegan via Struan. This is a 1960 view; MacPhie withdrew from bus operation in 1969.

Below right: MacBrayne's took over the Skye Transport business from SCWS in 1958, and among the seven vehicles which it acquired was this 1952 Albion Victor FT3AB with bodywork by Harvey. Seen in 1965, it was sold the following year.

Below: Skye Cars of Broadford operated a weekly summer service between Portree and Glasgow — southwards on Friday, northwards on Saturday. In July 1965 the vehicle was this Duple-bodied Bedford SB. Later in the 1960s the operation was taken over by Wallace Arnold Tours.

Above: In 1965 Carson of Dunvegan took over Nicholson's Skeabost Bridge service. The Carson fleet included this AEC Reliance with Duple (Midland) coach body which had been new in 1960 to Hutchison of Overtown. The three-figure phone number is a reminder of simpler days when long-distance calls still had to be routed through an operator. Carson's three-vehicle business was bought by MacBrayne's in 1970.

Right: An unusual type to find in Scotland was the Bristol SC4LK. This one, originally operated in Wales by Crosville, was in the fleet of MacLeod, Duntulm, in 1977.

Below right: Highland Omnibuses absorbed the bulk of the MacBrayne's bus operation in the early 1970s, acquiring the Skye operations in 1970/1. With them came this 1969 Bedford SB5 with Willowbrook body, which had been one of the last vehicles to be bought by MacBrayne's. It was photographed at Kyleakin in 1977.

Left: There have been few double-deckers based on Skye. Nicolson of Borve, which in 1981 took over the MacLeod business, operated school contracts, the reason for purchasing this Southdown Leyland Titan PD3 with that operator's characteristic Northern Counties body. It retained National Bus Company leaf-green livery, and, while the Southdown name was removed, the NBC logo remained.

Left: This former Highland Ford R-series with Duple Dominant body was purchased by Sutherland of Glenbrittle and is seen in 1988 on the Portree–Fiskavaig service, taken over from Macrae of Carbost in 1962.

Below: In the early 1980s Highland Omnibuses bought some new Leyland Leopards with Alexander Y-type bodywork. This 62-seater, however, was acquired from Alexander (Fife) in 1983. It is seen at Sligachan on its way to Portree from Kyleakin in 1988.

A LOOK BACK
AT BUSES

'The boundary lines have fallen for me in pleasant places'. It's not often we start articles on buses with quotes from scripture, but as a good non-conformist I can say a hearty 'Amen' to that quote from Psalm 16 v6. They have. Not many people have been able to sit on the sidelines and watch the unfolding drama of the bus industry over the last 20-odd years. I wouldn't have enjoyed being in the thick of it, fearing for my future or watching my pay and conditions being eroded in the interests of cutting public expenditure. I don't pretend — and never have pretended — to *like* everything that's happened to our beloved industry in that time. But spectating and commentating on it all has been fascinating.

My interest in buses dates back almost as far as I can remember, and Ian Allan publications have featured in our household throughout my life. Apparently as a little lad I couldn't ride anywhere on my tricycle until I had reached behind me to press the starter button.

Sad? Well, maybe, but when you were brought up in Manchester in the 1960s surely there couldn't be anything more interesting than the thousands of buses in every different hue. Most of my schoolmates would have heated discussions over the relative merits of strange people called Denis Law and George Best, and I well remember being thumped by a paper-boy early one morning

Stephen Morris hung up his boots as the longest-serving editor of *Buses* in 1999. Shamelessly self-indulgent, he recalls some of the aspects of his life there — and before — which captured his imagination.

Everything the well-equipped journalist needs: note-pad, pen, camera, champagne glass (sadly empty by this stage); Stephen Morris wonders whether the new Arriva low-floor DAF double-decker he's sitting on is going to be the answer to all London's transport ills. Later modifications were influenced in part by the doubts he was to express in the columns of *Buses*. Stuart Jones

on my way to school, not for supporting the wrong football team but for not supporting it sufficiently assiduously. I never remember thumping anybody for suggesting Salford's buses were better than Manchester's, however tempted I might have been.

All those wonderful liveries being swept away in an endless sea of orange was one of the more traumatic happenings of my existence, but nothing could remove my affection for and interest in the Manchester bus scene. I've now been in the south for more than half my life, but I still feel at home in Manchester, and to that extent it matters not that what would once have been a Crossley, a PD2 or a 'Mancunian' is now a Stagecoach Volvo — or even a MAN. At least I can use buses simply and easily in Manchester; it's ironic that moving to Shepperton to edit *Buses* was the first time I accepted that a car was a necessity, not a luxury.

I never had any intention of settling in northwest Surrey, despite three very happy years not far away at Royal Holloway College in Egham. It was then that I discovered that buses didn't run every few minutes and couldn't always be relied upon. True, we had quite interesting buses round Egham; the main service, the 441, was still run by green RMLs and, when one failed (they did sometimes, honestly!) you might get an RT. Further variety was provided by Alder Valley, with double-deck coaches passing by on commuter work and an occasional service which was often supplied by what looked like Bristol LHs but were in fact ECW-bodied Ford R1014s. Then there were vestiges of Royal Blue, in the form of National Express services 705 to Exeter (and sometimes extended to Perranporth — it sounded wonderful, but I hadn't a clue where it was!) and 721 to Bournemouth, still run more often than not by classic ECW-bodied Bristol RELHs, painted white but still pure Royal Blue on the inside. It was great to be able to stand outside the college and hop on such a classic vehicle to be whisked away to the coast or the West Country — or have a day in Winchester in the days between King Alfred and the Friends thereof.

More mundanely, we had five buses an hour into

Staines in those days, but what I could never understand was why three of those five all had to run together. It was apparently due to the need to make connections elsewhere on two long Green Line routes (and here was more variety, with

Top: **Southampton's East Lancs-bodied AEC Regents on routes such as the 17 were both a distraction and a useful means of transport in the days when Stephen Morris thought he might become a teacher. Failing that teaching practice, he reckons, was one of the best things he ever did.**

All photographs by the author except where indicated.

Above: **A London Coaches Leyland Titan on the 52 from Willesden at Victoria. Has there been a better bus since?**

RP-class Reliances, SMA-class Alexander-bodied Swifts and the odd RF). Yet, as far as I could see, the intention was to make sure that nothing ever connected with anything else, or gave anything approaching convenience to the passenger. It's an approach which seems to have been perpetuated to this very day round here. On a Sunday, for instance, we have a council-supported bus service between Shepperton and Walton-on-Thames that runs every two hours, on exactly the same timing as a BAA-supported service that runs every half hour. But who am I to understand the deep-rooted reasons which make this the case? I'm only a passenger.

It was never my intention to come back to the area, but life doesn't quite run as planned. A year in Southampton might have been more productive had it not been spent seeking out AEC Regent Vs, marvelling at strange ticket machines that took pictures of the money you inserted on immaculate cream and red Atlanteans, and looking for Hants & Dorset Bristol REs and strange Lodekkas, some of the unusual FL variety and some with wonderfully raucous Leyland engines coupled to screaming semi-automatic gearboxes. I was supposed to be studying to be a music teacher, but the music these things could emit was far more creative than the innovative educational music techniques which my tutor, a leading light in his field, was trying to instil into me. The only bright spot on the day when my final teaching practice collapsed about my ears in a mele of rioting eight-year-olds was the Regent V that took me home.

I had left Manchester in 1975, when the job market was booming. Now it was May 1979, and there just weren't jobs for a failed music teacher. Once I had been carefully profiled by the college's careers service, the only profession they could think of for me was as a careers adviser. Those that can, do, those that can't, teach . . . and those that can't teach advise the people that can do, what to do. They came up with only two other opportunities: peripatetic woodwind teacher on the Orkneys (I never got a reply to my query

Top: **Old lumbering Bristol VR meets the cheeky new minibus of the future in Exeter. It was to be this grown-up son of a Ford Cortina which was the bus of the future in 1983, not the Leyland Titan.**

Above: **Transits galore — minibus launch at Weston-super-Mare.**

as to whether a company boat was supplied) or in industrial relations with British Leyland at Longbridge. I can't think why *that* job was vacant . . .

But despair turned to vague hope when *Buses* was advertising for an assistant editor. The day of the interview dawned well; I waited for the bus to take me from Didsbury to get the train to Manchester Piccadilly, and a brand-new Leyland Titan hove into view. I had never previously managed to travel on one, and I marvelled at this masterpiece of sophistication. Ride quality and noise levels were like nothing I had ever encountered, those superb big windows . . . everything seemed just right about this bus. This was the future; the day when the whole country ran buses just like this could not come soon enough — but come it would, there was no doubt. There would be no turning the clock back now.

Surely this Titan was a good omen for how the day would go, and if I was going to be a bus journalist I'd better start now. I plucked up courage and asked the driver what he thought of his new bus. 'It's like a spaceship', he replied.

The interview seemed to go fine, apart from the fact that the elderly gentleman at the end of the row of interviewers, who had been introduced to me as John Parke, then editor of *Buses*, sat quietly and glowered disapprovingly throughout. Eventually it was his turn to interrogate me, and I quaked slightly in my shoes. 'What do you think of the Government's plans to deregulate the coach industry?' he asked. It so happened I had just read his editorial on the subject on the train. Obviously this callow youth from the sticks knew a bit about buses and wasn't a complete fool, and John and I chatted away. The glowering lifted, the twinkle in that disapproving eye became more prominent. It was the first of many long and very entertaining conversations I was to enjoy with this fount of all knowledge (and buses were only the tip of the iceberg where John Parke's encyclopædic brain was concerned). The rest of the interview panel grew restless, but John and I just ignored them. It looked like I might have got the job. I'd give it three years and then go back to Manchester, I reckoned.

John Parke taught me all I needed to know about producing a magazine, and in those days we

Below: **The all-conquering Dennis Dart; it could be a grown-up minibus or, like this one in Edinburgh, a slightly shrunken 'big bus'.**

produced *Buses* in a way which would have seemed quite familiar to Mr Caxton and would be totally alien to anyone involved in publishing today under the age of about 40. There was not a computer in sight: we bashed out copy on ancient typewriters, sent it off to be typeset in hot metal, sized up the pictures and sent them off to blockmakers. Several days later all these bits and pieces came together, we cut up the typeset galleys and 'pulls' of the blocks (ie the picture as it would appear in the magazine), stuck it all down with Cow Gum, which was as far as we went with designing the pages in those days, sent the whole lot back to the printers in Sawston (close to today's Showbus site at Duxford) and, with a bit of luck, printed magazines would come back a week or so later looking something like the way we hoped they would. Today magazines are produced all

electronically; there are no typesetters and no block makers, and we wonder how we managed without our trusty Apple Macs. But at least typewriters never 'crashed'.

Two weeks after I started, John Parke went off on holiday and left me to produce the December 1979 issue of *Buses* by myself; it was 'sink or swim' time.

It must have been a busy month, though hindsight doesn't recall life

Above right: **Stagecoach thrashed Volvo B10Ms up and down the motorways, though this one is on hire from Park's for a Glasgow–Inverness service.**

Right: **The new order: the Volvo B10M replaced the Leyland Leopard and AEC Reliance in the affections of many coach operators. Duple's high-floor Caribbean body aimed to follow the square-cornered look coming in from the likes of Van Hool, though its low-floor counterpart, the Laser, refined the curvaceous look preferred by British builders at the time.**

being as pressurised as it was to become later. But I compiled a feature on Park Royal, to mark the announcement of its closure, due in June 1980, and to make my mark it opened with a picture of the first 'Mancunian'. Then I went and had a look at a brand-new concept being shown in Britain for the first time, the 'pusher' artic. This was a left-hand-drive Mercedes-Benz O.305G, unusually for an artic at the time fitted with a rear engine, which involved complicated turntable systems to prevent jack-knifing. Mercedes had introduced the 'pusher' artic two years earlier, and was testing the reaction in Britain with a view to a possible right-hand-drive version. It would be another 20 years before the artic gained even limited acceptance.

In a way it's strange looking back to that December 1979 issue. Much has changed; there were new Bedfords, a new Metrobus on the cover, and operators were just showing an interest in a comparative newcomer — the Dennis Dominator — which marked its manufacturer's return to the bus scene. At this stage, though, volumes were still such that you couldn't be sure whether Dennis really had much of a future. Past experience indicated it probably hadn't.

In those days there was a column in *Buses* called 'Bus & Coach Developments' (someone managed to leave off the 's' in that December issue, but never mind) which culled material from licence applications, which also shows that things have changed. Flights Coach Services Ltd, Birmingham, had 'applied for summer express services from Newcastle upon Tyne to Nice and to Cerbere', with various pick-up points listed, and what we didn't say was that there would have been various 'backing' applications too — every traffic area through which it had to travel had to approve these 'backings'. Meanwhile Hants & Dorset Motor Services Ltd proposed 'timetable modifications and some service revisions in its Salisbury and Devizes operations'. Someone from those operators would have had to take time to prepare a case and go to the traffic courts to defend their applications. The whole thing seems like another age.

Yet, in this other world of Bedfords and traffic courts, my first editorial leader sympathised with operators 'facing a virtually impossible task of providing an efficient, economic service, whilst contending with staff shortages, congested roads . . .', which could just as easily have been written in 2001, even if it went on to mention the problems of obtaining new buses and spare parts — a problem happily behind us, at least on the scale then being experienced. But talk of how to attract the motorist back to buses also sounds so familiar from the perspective of a new millennium. *Plus ça change . . .*

Down the years since then I seem to have been held personally responsible for all sorts of things. One of the more difficult aspects of producing a magazine is maintaining balanced coverage, and at times one had to accept that 'balance' could not always be achieved from issue to issue, but had to be expressed over a much longer term. During my tenure of the post, the industry went through such huge change that things which at one time would

Left: **European-style double-deck coach from Plaxton: the Paramount 4000 was based initially on a Neoplan underframe and this was the first, for Excelsior. Both this and 'real' Neoplans were later offered with a Gardner engine — though not one based entirely on the 5LW.**

have seemed momentous became almost everyday occurrences. There were major topics which I felt had to be aired adequately, and at the time it was almost as if we had become obsessed with certain issues. Readers of more of a right-wing tendency than myself no doubt felt I had an obsession with 'bashing' the Transport Secretary of the day, Nicholas Ridley, at every opportunity, and I would have difficulty denying it. But I felt he deserved it and knew his skin was thick enough to take it.

At least in those days Government was keen to talk to the trade press, and I had quite a lot of contact with Ridley and his cohorts. Just to show I don't hate Tory MPs on principle, both Lynda Chalker and Tom King were always delightful to deal with, and the loss of Lynda as an MP left the country the poorer. And in later years I developed great respect for Steve Norris, which was nothing to do with the fact we almost shared a name. But then the first speech I heard him give included the word 'integration' several times — a concept which Ridley had dismissed as meaningless. That speech, incidentally, was given at the reopening of Victoria Coach Station after its major refurbishment, when the coach station authorities

were very keen to show us their posh backlit signs and information displays. What a shame it coincided with a power cut.

When coach deregulation came about the bias of the magazine swung away from good old-fashioned service buses to coaches, because that was where everything was happening. I passed my PSV test soon after coach deregulation, and I well remember thinking how unusual it was to be driving a service bus on one occasion, because I only ever seemed to drive coaches. Yet, in later years, after buses were deregulated, I was in trouble from the coach lobby for only covering service buses! Later, the same was true for minibuses, I was then accused of having some fetish for the Dennis Dart, and finally low-floor buses took over.

I'm convinced some readers felt I was personally responsible for many of these phenomena. But don't shoot the messenger! My aim was to reflect what was going on in the industry. Indeed, it can now be placed on record that I heartily dislike minibuses and I tolerate Dennis Darts. In both cases I can applaud the contribution they made to the bus industry. I can understand the tendency that dismisses minibuses as 'breadvans', but at the same time they represented a revolution in provision of urban bus services. They made travel easy, accessible (if not in the sense we now use the word) and fun in a way double-deckers never could. And the Dart in its turn made a massive contribution to the industry. It's passenger-friendly, driver-friendly, cheap to buy, cheap to run — and if you like *real* buses, very boring. Who cannot yearn for the healthy throb of a Leyland 680 or the song of a Daimler preselector gearbox when being subjected to the soulless buzzing of a Cummins B-series revving its head off in the back?

If I had to nominate a bus of the last 20 years or so which I considered to be the 'bee's knees', it would have to be the one which made my day when I went for my interview at Ian Allan — the Leyland Titan. It's not even a bus I've written about much, but when Gavin Booth and I decided in a burst of modernistic rebellion to test one for *Classic Bus* recently, it confirmed everything I thought of it in 1979. It was quite simply the best bus I had ever driven.

Coach deregulation duly took place on 6 October 1980. It was one of the first reforms of Margaret Thatcher's Government, and was almost a testing of the waters for liberalising and reducing public-sector involvement in so many aspects of life. Norman Fowler was Secretary of State for Transport at the time and had been the architect of

the 1980 Transport Act, and I was up bright and early to go and witness him heralding this brave new era by sinking slowly into the mud at what was laughably called King's Cross Coach Station to wave off the departure which signified the new régime, the first British Coachways service. However, as *Buses* reported at the time, it was public-sector Southend Transport that really ran the first deregulated coach journey, having set off earlier that morning.

King's Cross Coach Station was then an empty demolition site which is now the site of the British Library. Previously, Victoria Coach Station, in its pre-refurbishment form, had been reckoned to be one of the worst public buildings in London, but this sank to new depths. Almost literally.

British Coachways was a consortium of independent coach operators which set up a skeleton network to compete on major corridors with National Express. It was led by Grey-Green, whose Marketing Director Mike Kay shamelessly cribbed the contemporary image of British Airways

Opposite: **Volvo victorious: the last vestiges of Leyland disappear as the first Volvo Olympian rolls off the line at Irvine in March 1993.**

Below: **A fine performer when it went: a National Express Dennis Falcon/Duple Goldliner at its launch.**

— then, of course, still state-owned. The other participants were Ellerman Beeline, Morris Bros of Swansea, Park's of Hamilton, Shearings, Ribblesdale and Wallace Arnold, and the original network, based on King's Cross, served Bristol/Plymouth/Torbay, Cardiff/Swansea, Birmingham/Manchester/Liverpool/Glasgow, Sheffield/Barnsley/Leeds/Bradford and Middlesbrough/Newcastle.

Though that ceremonial first departure was by what purported to be a newly-delivered Grey-Green Duple-bodied Leyland Leopard, these independents were not tied to a state-owned British supplier, and could buy what they liked. By now the Leopard had been around for 20 years, from the early days of motorways, and though a good, solid workhorse with a top speed well in excess of 80mph, it was not ideal for long-distance motorway work. Its engine was noisy, its power-to-weight ratio and the spread of its gearbox ratios meant it would lose speed dramatically on long hills, and it had unsophisticated leaf springs. Indeed, on the 11m version, rear shock absorbers were an optional extra! Volvo and DAF were already showing the way, with more powerful coaches with more gear ratios (12, in the case of the DAF) and optional air suspension, soon to become standard. And Park's was to use German-built rear-engined integrals, MAN SR280s, on its London–Glasgow service.

It was almost the beginning of the end for British-built coaches. Before long, we had Bovas, Neoplans, Setras, Scanias, Van Hools etc joining the list of builders able to provide more suitable long-distance motorway coaches, while Van Hool, Berkhof and Jonckheere became more commonplace as bodybuilders, along with a string of other Continental hopefuls, many of them vanishing almost as quickly as they arrived.

It all made for interesting times, and even National Express had to start using similar coaches or see its market share eroded. The British responded, but the solid dependability and sophistication of the likes of the Volvo B10M had already won the hearts of many operators. Leyland, Plaxton and Duple all came up with new products, though Leyland's poor public perception by this time meant that most operators could see no reason to swap back from their new favourites,

and, as these came to be traded in, operators found the Volvo/Van Hool combination (in particular) held its value so well as to make initial higher costs worthwhile.

A fledgling company joining the fray called Stagecoach was typical of the Brave New World of express coaching; brand-new Volvos were put on the road and pounded up and down the motorway all day and all night, stopping occasionally for a quick service, a wash and to have the toilet emptied.

So what became of the British coach industry? State-owned National Express fought back, aided by an easily-identifiable image, wider network and better, well-established terminal facilities — though questions were often asked (and carefully skirted round) about its financial performance at press conferences to announce National Bus Company annual reports. Because National Express operations were an integral part of the various bus companies' operations, you couldn't really look at them in isolation and it was very difficult to single out their financial performance — this was the sort of stock reply we got to our questions. Whatever bearing this had, National Express emerged triumphant, but the British coach manufacturers were now holed below the waterline. Bedford and Ford made lightweight vehicles which were even less well-suited to sustained, fast running and mileages often exceeding 100,000 a year, and pulled out. Leyland was a spent force, though you wouldn't have thought so from the Tiger's début in Tangiers — far and away the most elaborate vehicle launch I attended in 20 years — and Britain's coach-bodybuilding industry had so much over-capacity that only the takeover of Duple by its arch rival Plaxton enabled anything to be rescued.

The withdrawal of Bedford and Ford coincided with Dennis's launch of a new medium-weight mid-engined chassis, the Javelin. We possibly didn't realise then what a hugely significant vehicle that would be.

Dennis had had other stabs at the coach market. The Dominator was to become all things to all men, and by stretching it and putting the engine in line it could make a coach and a single-deck bus. Dennis, of course, was involved in the manufacture of fire tenders and municipal vehicles too. Perkins V8 engines worked well in fire engines, and they were very powerful, fast-revving and smooth units to boot — perfect for coaches. Meanwhile, NBC had thrown down the challenge for a British-built high-floor, rear-engined coach to be ready to roll in six months as a competitor to all

Above opposite: **A prototype Lance chassis takes shape in Dennis's development shop.**

Below opposite: **A new Dennis Dorchester for Western Scottish.**

these foreign Johnnies. Duple offered the high-floor Goldliner body, and this strange hybrid of Dominator bus chassis, fire-engine driveline and high-specification coach body emerged as the Falcon V. Dennis knew a thing or two about ride quality, and the low centre of gravity from using what was effectively a double-deck bus chassis contributed to a good ride; the Perkins lived up to its promise of being smooth, quiet and powerful, while the Duple body was the height of luxury.

Hindsight tells us the Falcon V was (as my successor Alan Millar would say) a 'blunderbus' — spectacularly so, all the more because it was the most high-profile exercise Dennis had been involved in at a critical phase of the company's development. It's not easy to establish credibility in the coach business, and Dennis was not doing well in this respect. Had those Falcons proved the equal of a Neoplan or a Volvo, Dennis might have had it made. But for what was still a small company (in automotive terms) to develop a premium, heavyweight coach in six months was too tall an order.

From my personal point of view, NBC's Falcons were quite superb. I made a number of long-distance trips on them, and every time they performed faultlessly; they were amongst the most comfortable and swiftest coaches on the road at the time. But, unlike many, I was never dumped on the hard shoulder by one. It was a classic case of well-tried components being used in unfamiliar

Above: The Javelin approach of using bought-in components was to lead to a whole range of new models, of which perhaps the ultimate is the Trident. A Stagecoach Selkent 'short' one leaves West Croydon.

Above: The low-floor revolution begins. *Buses* was invited to an exclusive preview of Wright's development Pathfinder. So had been several other bus and coach journalists, and the company's attempts to keep them from discovering each other in Ballymena and its environs were even more memorable than the preview itself! In the end the pretence was given up, and we shared this particular 'exclusive preview' amicably with Mike Morgan of *Coach & Bus Week*.

settings. The Voith gearbox, for instance, is excellent in a service bus but is not designed for sustained high-speed running. The Perkins V8 works fine in the front of a fire engine, but less well at the back of a coach when insufficient development time has been made available. And the Duple body, no problem on a mid-engined Volvo, did not sit quite so well on a rear-engined bus chassis. Maybe with more time and development resources it would have worked.

More cross-fertilisation came with the Lancet, which was actually derived from Dennis's dustcart production, which will probably be of little surprise to anyone who has travelled on one of the short ones built for Portsmouth. I well remember the launch outside Portsmouth's Guildhall of this rather pretty little bus, which was memorable for its dreadful ride quality; it was like a little bucking bronco. But Dennis was developing a bigger coach — the Dorchester — with optional air suspension and a horizontal Gardner engine, which turned it into quite an acceptable vehicle, albeit amongst a very select group of clients.

So would the Javelin be any better? It's unfair to suggest the Javelin only succeeded because Bedford and Ford had pulled out of the market. The Javelin showed innovation, in that by using a compact Cummins C-series engine fitted as close as possible to the rear axle you could put a big underfloor luggage locker within the wheelbase *and* have the traditional boot of a mid-engined coach.

What was significant was the way it changed Dennis's approach. If you went to Bedford or Ford you got a chassis that Bedford or Ford wanted to produce. If you went to Dennis and wanted something slightly different they would make it for you. A South Yorkshire Dominator may have little in common with, say, a Leicester one. Surely, that's as it should be: a bespoke bus for a bespoke operation? Well, yes. Until you want spare parts for it. Or until Steeple Bumpstead Corporation's patent gland-stuffing grommet makes it drop all its engine oil in the middle of the High Street. The Javelin was a Javelin — take it or leave it. Thus engineering costs could be devoted to things that mattered, and you could phone the parts supplier and be sure of getting the bit that would fit your

Below: **Optare's innovation was to show itself in vehicles like this Spectra demonstrator. Whatever happened to J382 BNW? In this view it appeared in Battersea Park for the finals of the 1991 London Bus Driver of the Year, at which one S. Morris was the commentator.**

Above : **Another new Optare — one of the very first Excels, on its launch trip in Blackpool.**

carried out in a tiny corner of Dennis's huge old factory in Guildford, looking very forlorn in acres of emptiness. Now Dennis has a new factory on the outskirts of town which is always filled to capacity and a hive of activity — full not just with vehicles destined for every corner of Britain, but with export products going way beyond even its traditional Hong Kong market, to Canada, the United States, the Netherlands and Portugal. On my last visit, it was even building double-deckers for Spain — and Birmingham! Travel West Midlands had been one of the last bastions of non-Dennis land. And, by this time, Dennis had joined forces with Plaxton and Alexander to create TransBus International, something I had never seen in my 20 years at *Buses* — a major British-based European bus builder.

Dennis was not the only builder to survive against the odds. When Roe's Plant Director Russell Richardson, with help from the West Yorkshire Enterprise Board, decided to take over his factory when Leyland closed it down in 1984, I was convinced his venture was doomed to failure. Bus Grant had gone, the industry was battening down the hatches to survive privatisation and deregulation, and the market slumped. The industry needed another manufacturer like a hole in the head. Richardson's new company was called Optare, and started off with box-like bodies on the Leyland Cub and another Dennis Dominator derivative, the Domino midi. These were built for sympathetic Yorkshire-based public-sector operators, while the closure of ECW at about the same time meant that it was allowed for a time to build the Leyland-group body under licence on the Olympian.

But Optare was to show tremendous design flair once it had got off the ground, combining the innovation of a brand-new company with the experience and expertise of some of the old

vehicle, not someone else's special. All in all, it made for a much more reliable vehicle and cut production costs. It wasn't quite the equal of a B10M in terms of performance and refinement, but it wasn't bad; it was excellent on fuel consumption, it was a sight more reliable than those Falcons, and it was a great vehicle to drive. Dennis was about to move into the big time.

The Javelin has waxed and waned in popularity over the years and in not a few of those years it has been a very serious contender in the coach market. It's probably true to say that the Javelin laid the foundation for Dennis's subsequent successes. The combination of computer-aided design and clever engineering in bringing together readily available and well-proven units has enabled Dennis to gain that credibility which for so long eluded it in building products that really work, and innovation has been used to second-guess what the market really wants.

The 1980s were a very sad time for British bus manufacturing; one of the gloomier aspects of editing *Buses* over those 20 years was having to report the demise of so many well-known and well-loved names — like Park Royal, in my very first issue. I well remember seeing bus production

Charles H. Roe workforce. It was to be a winning combination, and Optare has survived against the odds, supplying innovative products largely to companies in the mid-range of the industry — those not under pressure to buy massive batches of buses at the lowest price they can get, yet large enough and concerned enough about their image to buy buses that make a statement.

Both Dennis and Optare represented approaches to the newly commercialised market brought in by Nicholas Ridley and which were to bring about such fundamental change to everything in the bus industry. One day I shall write a book about it, and, as I expect Mr Editor Brown will want to fit a few other articles into this Yearbook, I'd better refrain from embarking further on that subject.

I still can't bring myself to agree that the free-market approach to buses has been A Good Thing. My visits to Manchester now give me experience of excellent, high-frequency bus services; there is (on some corridors) genuine choice between price and quality — though, where bus operation is concerned, is this not little more than an academic exercise? Readers of *Buses Yearbook* may enjoy a ride on a bus for the sake of it, but for most people it is a means to an end, and the quicker the journey is out of the way, the better. Most people want to

be able to get on the first bus that comes, and won't wait in the hope that a more comfortable one (or even a cheaper one) will come along soon. And today's Manchester bus scene comes after years of chaos which decimated passenger numbers.

On the other hand, my dear friends at Arriva have cut off my choice of whether to use the car or the bus when I want to visit Ian Allan at Hersham; a bus link going back at least 75 years has been severed recently, and the operator didn't even have the decency to tell the passengers. That's the downside of the new régime. At the same time, the rest of Europe must have been incredulous at the recent antics with our railways, and you have to question whether over the last 20 years we have followed the right path with our transport 'policies'.

I think I know what my answer to that question would be, but I'd hate to be accused of political bias . . .

Below: **Deregulation as it's supposed to be? Market egmentation gives you a cheap ride down Wilmslow Road on a Stagecoach Manchester MagicBus Atlantean (since replaced by Dennis Dragons repatriated from Kenya) or an expensive ride on a newer Volvo B10M.**

THIS IS
THE BBC...

Ever dreamed of starting your own bus company . . . ? Martin S. Curtis has, and here's his story.

I f anyone imagines that a group of bus company managers, each with more than 20 years' experience, could easily establish a completely *new* operating company, the answer is that it isn't quite that simple! Nor, however, is it impossible, despite the lack of an established base and considerable competition from existing bus operators.

So it was, towards the end of 1996, that the idea of Bath Bus Company Ltd came into being. The very name suggested a long-established operator, which probably dominated the local transport scene, and of course the initials were certainly familiar to almost everyone, for quite a different reason. But in fact there had never been a Bath Bus Company before, as the Bath companies engaged in bus operation during earlier years were tramways-company-related, themselves having been controlled by the Bristol Tramways organisation from the mid-1930s. Finding a name

for the new company was therefore the easy part, and allowed the company to be quickly recognised locally.

Initially, open-top tour-bus work was the main target for breaking into the market place, and, since overseas visitors still think 'red' when it comes to British double-deckers, standard Post Office red was chosen as the main fleet colour. This was relieved by a bright primrose, which had been developed in an earlier situation for tour buses and was known to stand out well from the crowd.

The procedure for actually commencing operation proved far more difficult. The four individuals involved in the establishment of the company had considerable experience in operations, engineering and the finances of bus companies. What was lacking were vehicles and a base, and so efforts were made to acquire another small bus company locally, from which to develop the business. One such operator which was willing to sell was found, and after several months of

A view of the ex-Cardiff Alexander-bodied Bristol VRT open-topper, taken from the BBC offices overlooking Bath city centre. All photographs by the author

Above: A former Southern Vectis open-top VRT stands alongside the ex-Cardiff bus. Although wearing the company's original Sightseeing livery, both carry the new City Sightseeing insignia.

negotiations all was set for the takeover, which had been reported at length in the local press. Then, without warning, the established operator withdrew from the deal, three days before completion was due.

Many preparations had already been made, including raising the necessary financial backing and making an application for an operator's licence. The latter had appeared in *Notices and Proceedings* during January 1997 (much to the consternation of the local major-group operator, which had formerly employed the new BBC board!). It was nevertheless decided to proceed alone and establish from scratch a new operation, while the small operator which was to have been acquired would remain now as a competitor.

The acquisition of open-top buses commenced — four vehicles initially, three of which were to be Bristol VRTs, converted and painted by three of the directors, under the strict supervision of the engineer. A fourth bus — an AEC Routemaster already converted to open-top and previously with London Coaches — was supplied by Blue Triangle ready-painted in Bath Bus Company's new colours. The RM disgraced itself by breaking down with an engine-valve defect on its delivery run from London.

The first two VRs and later the RM made lengthy excursions to Newtown, Powys, where Actia computerised multi-lingual commentary equipment was fitted. Similar systems were fitted to all the company's open-toppers, but later buses were fitted-out in Bath. However, whilst the use of a live guide remained an option, this commentary equipment was very sophisticated and enabled information to be conveyed to passengers in up to seven languages simultaneously, even if the bus

was delayed in traffic or left its usual route. This offered a unique feature not available on any of the other three, established open-top bus tours already running in Bath, against which the BBC would compete.

On 20 May 1997 the first two Bristol VRs took to the streets, using an excursion licence. The Routemaster followed within a week, but, by the time the third VR was introduced in June, a fully-registered, hop-on/ hop-off service was in place. This commenced in Bath's High Street near the Abbey and Roman Baths, and resulted in problems, since the other three companies each had a street sales stand approved by the local council. Due to objections raised by the other bus companies (well they would, wouldn't they?), such a stand was refused in a suitable location for the BBC and, at the time of writing, four years later, this matter has never been resolved.

The other operators also made complaints about alleged obstruction at High Street bus stops, even though their tours commenced elsewhere. This resulted in some confusion among a few local traffic wardens, who believed BBC vehicles should not stop at this location and sought to move buses on as they attempted to load. Furthermore, two of the rival operators then parked their own buses in an attempt to block BBC vehicles at bus stops, which exacerbated the situation. We will return to this aspect later.

It was always the intention to expand the business beyond tour buses, although it was tour trade that provided the much needed initial revenue. This was also an important political point, since local councillors and others wanted a new bus company to break an otherwise virtual monopoly on local routes. However, they were uncomfortable about more tour buses, which were already controversial with many residents, who (among other things) didn't like being stared at by tourists. The closure of Royal Crescent to tour buses a few years later had much to do with this view, as well as protection of the environment.

From the autumn of 1997, four school-bus contracts commenced, having been awarded by the local authority. Two of these required coaches, while two needed double-deck buses. Three Volvo B10M coaches were purchased for this work, together with more VRTs which were hurriedly prepared with little testing before going into service. The coach contracts went well for the next three years until the company decided to move away from school-contract work, as it made limited use of vehicles and staff. A close working relationship had developed with the schools in question, some lasting friendships were made, and (perhaps most surprisingly) some of the pupils themselves later

became BBC employees as the need arose for sales staff — or conductors on the RM.

The double-deck contracts didn't go so well. A main dealer had been responsible for vehicle servicing and much maintenance work in the early days of the company. This was not only costly, but the failure to meet deadlines was especially disappointing. The commencement of the school contracts saw some of the VRs suffering from breakdowns, so hiring-in became necessary. So bad did the situation become that, on one afternoon, open-top buses were employed following consultation with the school in question, although it is stressed that pupils only travelled on the lower deck, and two staff members were on each bus.

Action taken to resolve these problems swiftly took effect, but the damage had been done. Added to which, the local education department made the outrageous suggestion that a 14-year-old boy had driven one of the afternoon school buses, as

Below: **In July 1999, a Plaxton-bodied Volvo B10M fights through Wells Road traffic to enter the city, in what should be a bus lane. It is operating a morning peak C3 service from Peasedown.**

reported by an anonymous member of the public. The bus in question had in fact been driven by a rather petite — but full PCV-licence-holding — female member of staff, which resulted in some embarrassment! The double-deck school bus runs ceased, however; the services were converted to coaches with seatbelts, and taken over by other concerns.

The Bath Bus Company's aim was to introduce a commercial local bus service, and the loss of the double-deck school contracts released vehicles for a potential commercial bus route. The areas decided upon were Foxhill and Combe Down village, which were to be linked in a way that did not parallel an existing bus service, and provided new connections for residents, including to the commercial centre at the top of the city. An extensive house-to-house publicity campaign advised residents of the new service, to be numbered S1, and money-off vouchers ensured considerable support from the first day of operation — Saturday 15 November 1997.

Extensive passenger counts at the roadside were part of the main competitor's response to the new Foxhill route, which revealed many people boarding S1 buses near the shopping centre for the journey back to their homes, while few passengers seemed to travel in to town with the BBC. Presumably the larger company eventually realised that most passengers disembarked at the rear of the railway station and walked through a pedestrian way, while the buses looped around the city, before reaching their principal re-loading point!

With the commencement of this local service, the Bath Bus Company started to be taken much more seriously. Nevertheless, problems of finding a suitable base for all the company's vehicles, together with appropriate maintenance facilities, continued to cause difficulties.

Vehicles were parked overnight in various locations, but premises in Brassmill Lane, Bath, which had hitherto been a car-breakers' yard, were eventually acquired, together with a strip of land from an adjacent property. Without the latter, buses could not gain access to the parking area at the rear of the buildings, which, whilst far from ideal as bus workshops, provided a temporary solution until

the site could be properly redeveloped — or so it was thought at the time. However, at least in-house maintenance could commence with far less reliance on the main dealer for routine repairs and servicing.

The year 1998 opened with the company already running open-top tours, school coaches and a commercial service to Foxhill, but buses continued to be parked at locations as far apart as Box, Peasedown St John, Warmley and Bristol, in some cases using hauliers' and other coach operators' premises. Meanwhile the local authority failed to support a series of proposals and applications to improve the Brassmill Lane premises.

Ten vehicles were now owned but still could not

The second generation of Dennis Darts in the fleet carry 'LO-ENTRY' lettering and usually work on city services to Foxhill.

be garaged at one location. Accordingly, if a bus failed to start on any particular morning, the nearest replacement was likely to be at least 20 minutes away, which could seriously disrupt the first journeys of the day. The complications of driver scheduling from so many locations also became a nightmare during this period.

Another open-top VRT, in superb condition, was acquired from Southern Vectis on the Isle of Wight, while an existing covered-top VRT was converted to open-top during July. Later still, a convertible-open-top VRT with rare Alexander bodywork was

Bath Bus Company minibuses are Mercedes-Benz 609s and were acquired to operate council contracted services. This one is seen in Bath's High Street, where traffic wardens often insist that the company's vehicles move on.

acquired from Cardiff, which allowed one of the original open-top VRTs to be withdrawn.

The local council, meanwhile, granted the company an open-top sales stand near the tour's commencing point in the High Street. Near, but not *that* near. It was just possible to see the top of the bus parked on its stop, 50 yards or so down the street from the sales position.

Not surprisingly, potential passengers wanted the confidence of knowing they could board the bus where they bought their ticket (as was the case with all the other bus companies' sales stands), so the rent for the sales position generally exceeded any ticket sales taken at this location. Some changes were made to the High Street road markings too, and this prompted further activity from traffic wardens, who sent BBC buses around the block rather than permit them to wait on their stop — as, once again, was allowed for all the rival open-top buses. Despite this, BBC tour loadings increased, the popularity of a choice of language, the use of headphones and increased marketing resulting in BBC Sightseeing's becoming well-known.

Bath Bus Company then opened a small office in the city centre for administrative purposes, since the company's growing activities had brought with

them an increased level of office activity. A new administration and commercial manager had joined the company, having been a former colleague of the existing managers, and another former colleague became a fifth director. No longer was it necessary to undertake cash-counting on vehicles or deal with correspondence from a briefcase in a 'caff'. The office was a real boon, and had the added advantage of overlooking the city-centre stops of the rival tour-bus operators!

Some criticism had been levelled at the company for running old worn-out buses on its local service, and this was addressed during August 1998 when the first two Dennis Darts appeared in the fleet, on contract hire from Cheshire Bus & Coach (soon to be renamed Mistral). At a stroke, these vehicles transformed the local-service image to one offering very modern buses indeed.

By the end of that summer another new commercial service had been inaugurated, this time reaching outside of the city to the rapidly expanding village of Peasedown St John. Here, coaches were generally employed on an hourly service which included a new housing development that was still in the course of construction. This service was numbered C3 and did particularly well from the new estate, as it provided the only regular public transport link to the area.

Less successful was the S4 city service to Elmhurst Estate in Bath, via the London Road. With an hourly headway, it was considered by many to be too infrequent, while by the end of 1998 the major competing company — for the first time, surprisingly — was beginning to cut its own fares in areas where BBC buses were appearing, in an attempt to recover lost trade.

Some minor contract work for South Gloucestershire Council was undertaken using the Darts, to Marshfield during evenings and Sundays — although this was short-lived — while there was further activity in finding a BBC depot. By now the company was growing in popularity with the travelling pubic — and council members declared their desire to offer support. However, the reality of the situation was that every idea for providing parking in the city, even in industrial areas, was turned down — usually after very lengthy periods of debate during which there was no decision at all. Among the sites rejected was a yard leased to the BBC by the council itself, near the Brassmill Lane workshops, and adjacent to the yard of one of the other tour-bus operators. After lengthy consideration, it was decided this plan would detract from the historic character of Bath and was rejected — although council members did tell officers to assist the BBC to find an alternative. They never did.

The much reported saga of the difficulties in finding a depot for the company appeared in *The Bath Chronicle*, the city's local daily newspaper, which indicated that the company

could close if a base was not found. As a result, an approach was made to the company from Burnett Business Park, remotely located outside the city on the Bristol side. Whilst situated outside Bath, it was decided to establish a bus park here from May 2000, with workshop facilities also being transferred to Burnett shortly afterwards, following the sale of the Brassmill Lane premises. At last, all the company's vehicles and workshops were based at one location.

Meanwhile difficulties continued with traffic wardens who attempted to stop BBC vehicles from picking up passengers in the High Street. On one occasion the crew of the Routemaster, operating on its correct, registered service time, received a parking ticket while setting down and picking up passengers at one of the High Street bus stops! The company decided not to pay the fine, and instead took the matter to court. The case was dropped a few days before it was due to be heard.

By this time, the company's fleet had doubled, to 20 buses and coaches. Three Mercedes-Benz 609 minibuses had been introduced from April 1999 to

Below: **The manoeuvrability of the 67-seat Bendy buses is surprisingly good. Here one negotiates Terrace Walk at speed. This vehicle still carries its original registration C113 HDT, though all three BBC articulated buses later received BBZ ('bee bee zee', in the American style of pronunciation) marks.**

operate council-contracted Monday to Saturday services between Bath and Hinton Blewett, via Norton Radstock and many villages in between. This route included some very narrow twisting lanes barely wide enough even for a minibus. On Sundays, the same minibuses were employed on four city services across the City of Bath itself. The Norton Radstock area was also increasingly served by the C3 service, which was growing in popularity and, in various stages, was extended to Radstock and Midsomer Norton. With support from Somerset County Council, some C3 journeys also reached Shepton Mallet.

From November 1999 the S1 service was modified and expanded to offer an alternative S2 service to Foxhill via Odd Down. By this time the Mistral Darts had been replaced by low-floor versions which were most popular, particularly among parents with young children in pushchairs, of whom there were many travelling in this area. The Odd Down service soon became by far the most popular route to Foxhill, that via Combe Down having lost patronage in favour of a re-routed and more frequent rival service.

During 2000, the company took two further major steps. The first was its joining of the City Sightseeing consortium, resulting in the appearance of BBC open-top buses in a completely revised Bath City Sightseeing livery. This consortium is a worldwide organisation which links tour-bus operators around the globe and strengthens the combined travel arrangements for tourists wishing to move from city to city.

The second notable step was the bold decision to take three articulated vehicles into its fleet, principally for use on the C3 service, where loadings, especially in the morning peak, were growing and high-capacity vehicles were required. Whilst double-deckers could offer the capacity sought, the unusual availability of what the company marketed vigorously as 'BBC BENDY' buses offered a unique opportunity to make this service even more prominent. These buses certainly did that, and, while their length can sometimes result in difficulties in Bath city centre, this is outweighed by their impact in increasing public awareness of the company and its services. The articulated buses were previously in service with First Mainline of Sheffield, and now compete with services of the Bath operator which is a member of the same group as their previous owners.

Company development continues, as do many difficulties. One afflicting all operators in Bath — and in many other locations — is a shortage of suitable staff. This problem alone can restrict expansion, but as this is written, at the beginning of 2001, plans are in place for further service developments. And with the renewal of many council contracts due later in the year, further opportunities also exist in this area.

The purchase of further vehicles is being considered. The City Sightseeing connections are being continually strengthened, while there is speculation as to whether this is the year the company will be granted an open-top bus sales-stand *next* to a waiting position.

Meanwhile, a traffic warden closely inspects one of the company's vehicles and starts writing in his pad... .

Above opposite. **The entire open-top fleet as it was at the end of the 2000 summer season. Two vehicles already carry the new City Sightseeing livery.**

Below opposite: **The first bus to carry Bath City Sightseeing livery was this Bristol VRT which was a Cambus vehicle prior to open-top conversion to by Bath Bus Company.**

VEHICLES OWNED BY BATH BUS COMPANY AS AT JANUARY 2001

Mercedes 609D	E461/71/77 CGM
	F982 EDS
	F757 GUS
AEC/Park Royal Routemaster	783 DYE
Bristol VRT/ECW	NCD 563M
	232 ENX (*PHE 816M*)
	NFB 115R
	WOI 8022 (*PVO 818R*)
	UFX 857S
	XRR 176S
	BCL 213T
	KKK 888V
	JWV 252W
Bristol VRT/Alexander	WTG 360T
Volvo B10M/Plaxton	E282 OMG
	TJI 1682
Volvo B10M/Van Hool	PJI 3748 (*D848 KVE*)
Dennis Dart/Northern Counties	M387/9 KVR
Dennis Dart SLF/Plaxton	N606 WND
	P741/2/8 HND
Leyland-DAB artic	BBZ 6818 (*C113 HDT*)
	BBZ 8027 (*C112 HDT*)
	BBZ 8051 (*C111 HDT*)

HEROES

AND VILLAINS

What do these men have in common — Brian Souter, Groucho Marx, G. J. Rackham, Ian Allan, Buddy Holly, Moris Little, Spike Milligan, R. Stuart Pilcher, Alan Townsin, Neil Sedaka and Frank Pick? On the surface, probably very little — but their common denominator is that they are all heroes of mine. They don't know that — several of them never can — but the essence of hero-worship is that it should be from afar. Come on — surely you've had heroes; those people you admire and who have had some sort of influence on your life.

My friends will not be surprised at the absence of, say, sportsmen and politicians from the list in the paragraph above, even though I was at school with the (current at the time of writing) Foreign Secretary. No, I got to know my heroes through radio, 7in records and films, and, of course, through the pages of magazines like *Buses Illustrated* and *Bus & Coach*, and through the few books that were available to us info-hungry bus enthusiasts in the 1950s.

I could bore you for hours on the subject of Messrs Holly, Marx, Milligan and Sedaka, but my friend the editor insists that this book has to be about buses, so the list reduces. For an impressionable teenager in the late 1950s there weren't stalls groaning under the weight of bus books at preserved bus rallies. In fact, there weren't even rallies, come to think of it, because there were hardly any preserved buses to take to them.

Apart from the aforementioned *Buses Illustrated* — *BI* to generations of enthusiasts — there were a few bus books on the market. So few that we could count them and still have fingers to spare, and they almost inevitably showed an understandable bias towards London and fleets southern. That wasn't

too much of a problem because we were glad to get our hands on anything in print about buses. It was only later that those of us on the UK's Celtic fringes started to agitate for more local coverage, and some of us put our pens where our mouths were and helped to kick-start a broader interest by writing about local matters for the transport press — yes, even when we were in our teens.

It was in one of the few books from that era — the 1956-published *London General* — that I first learned about Frank Pick. The book was published by London Transport to commemorate the centenary of the first London General horse buses in 1856, and was read and re-read, often in preference to Latin homework. I had experienced London Transport at first hand on a family Coronation-year (1953) trip, and quickly came to

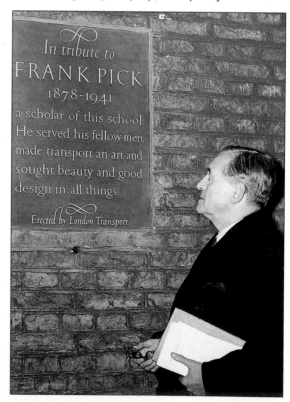

A memorial to Frank Pick at St Peter's School, York, being unveiled by Lord Latham in 1957.
London Transport

Frank Pick was keen on providing good passenger facilities, like this roadside shelter in Horse Guards Avenue in 1935.
London Transport

admire the care that went into creating and maintaining what we would later call a corporate identity.

LT's close attention to design — hopefully something that the new Transport for London organisation will continue — didn't happen by accident. Just because an undertaking like LT affects the lives of millions of people every day doesn't mean that it will be done well, or that there will be any sense of identity or consistency. A look at other European capitals, even today, dramatically demonstrates just how far advanced LT was more than 60 years ago. And while it's not all down to Frank Pick, he set the ball rolling when, as Vice-Chairman and Chief Executive of London Transport under Lord Ashfield, he founded the tradition that good design is an integral part of the provision of good service. As he said in a 1916 lecture, 'The test of the goodness of a thing is its fitness for use. If it fails on this first test, no amount of ornamentation finish will make it any better; it will only make it more expensive and more foolish.'

It is Frank Pick we must thank not only for things like the graphic clarity of all LT's notices and signs, but also for the splendid tradition of commissioning posters from the best artists of the day, and building stations and garages that are still regarded as design classics. And this same close attention to design is reflected in the design of London's buses, particularly through the 1930s, with a steady flow of mould-breaking types like the STL, 10T10, CR, TF and — of course — RT. Pick's design policy also included station furniture and moquettes. It would be unfair on other operators to imply that only London Transport had this enlightened approach to design, but nobody else achieved the impact that LT did.

I found out about R. Stuart Pilcher in a different way. Delving into the history of transport in Edinburgh, his was a name that kept cropping up. He was the city's Transport Manager from 1918 to 1928 — a man with the task of taking Edinburgh's municipal transport forward under direct Corporation control; until 1919 the tramway system had been leased to the Edinburgh & District Tramways company, but at the end of the lease control returned to the Corporation's hands.

R. Stuart Pilcher came to Edinburgh from Aberdeen, and inherited a tramway system that was cable-driven, while the rest of the world — and especially the adjacent Leith and Musselburgh systems — were electric and therefore incompatible. The cable system had become a joke, and Pilcher set about improving the fleet and planning for electrification. He invested in buses too — firstly touring charabancs, but then single-deck buses to serve areas beyond the tramlines.

Leith was amalgamated with Edinburgh in 1920, so the first electrification project in 1922 allowed electric cars to run through from Leith into the centre of Edinburgh. The whole cable-electric conversion was completed by 1923, and, while there was much investment in new trams, the bus fleet had grown to 130 by 1928, when Pilcher left Edinburgh to take up the prestigious post of General Manager of Manchester Corporation, where he set about replacing trams and mounted a staunch (but ultimately doomed) campaign to encourage the city to go straight to diesel motor buses and forget trolleybus operation.

Pilcher was one of the most respected busmen of his time, and went on to become Traffic Commissioner for the Midland Traffic Area. When he retired he returned to live near Edinburgh, and it was here in his later years that I briefly met him. He had been invited to a coach exhibition mounted by Scottish Omnibuses in its New Street depot in Edinburgh in 1958, and I realised who he was. So I did what any 15-year-old would have done — I plucked up courage to speak to him, and even got his autograph! I don't know what he thought about this schoolboy asking for his autograph, but if he was bemused by it all he didn't show it.

Frank Pick and R. Stuart Pilcher are heroes because of the important part they played in the development of the motorbus — Pick with his close interest in the importance of good design, Pilcher for his strong views and, of course, for his work setting Edinburgh Corporation on the right road.

G. J. Rackham falls into the same category as Pick and Pilcher. He was, of course, the legendary engineer who, as Chief Engineer for Leyland Motors, was responsible for the Tiger and Titan models that revolutionised bus design when they were launched in 1927. Combining low build and low weight with a beefy six-cylinder engine produced landmark models that were to influence everything that came after.

George John Rackham had an impressive career, starting with the Vanguard company in London, quickly becoming Chief Draughtsman of the London General company, and then moving to David Brown Ltd before returning to LGOC at Walthamstow. LGOC used the former Vanguard premises at Walthamstow to build its own buses, leading to the birth of the Associated Equipment Company — AEC — and, although Rackham's career took him to the United States as Chief Engineer of the Chicago-based Yellow Coach company before he returned to the UK in 1926 as

Right: **An example of Frank Pick's influence — London Transport's Hemel Hempstead garage, 1935.** London Transport

Opposite: **A rare sighting of Alan Townsin, then public relations officer for the West Midlands PTE.** WMPTE

Leyland's Chief Engineer, he stopped in Lancashire only long enough to develop the Tiger/Titan ranges before returning south to AEC as Chief Engineer.

Some say that he did so to escape the North West's climate, but, whatever the reason, AEC must have been pleased to have him, for he went on to design the Regal and Regent, which, with the Tiger and Titan, would dominate the bus market in the 1930s and for the next 30 years. By the time Rackham retired in 1950, just as the underfloor-engined Regal IV was appearing, he had steered AEC through more than two significant decades in the company's history, and had certainly played an important part in its undoubted success. As a Leyland fan, I'm only sorry that Rackham didn't stay longer in Lancashire, but nobody could question his influence on the design of British buses.

While Rackham is a hero, I suspect he's even more of a hero to another of my heroes — if you follow me. Many of us know about Rackham through the writings of Alan Townsin, who worked at AEC, but not under Rackham, and later turned his hand to journalism, with great success. Alan Townsin had the foresight to meet and interview John Rackham, giving the rest of us an opportunity to learn more about the great man through his subsequent writings. For many enthusiasts of a certain age, Alan Townsin is best remembered as editor of *Buses Illustrated*, the magazine that confirmed that there were indeed other people out there with this strange interest in buses. We learned much from *BI*, and some of us went on to become contributors.

It was Alan who published my first photos and my first paid-for attempts at journalism — a history of Alexanders coachworks that appeared when I was still at school. Forty years later and Alan is still active as a freelance, writing a string of invaluable (and constantly consulted) reference works as well as writing for magazines such as my own *Classic Bus*. I am delighted to be able to return the favour by commissioning articles from Alan, whose depth of knowledge and clear writing style makes his work a joy to read and indeed to edit. A few years ago, a small group of bus writers got together to surprise Alan with a dinner on the occasion of his 70th birthday, and it's reassuring to know that the Townsin word-processor is still much in use.

Ian Allan is a hero, and not just because his company is publishing this book and has published most of my books. Back in 1942, the young IA advertised his first listing of Southern Railway locomotives; the fact that he worked for the railway at the time did not go down well with some of his bosses, and he was ordered not to publish the booklet. He did, and cunningly sent a copy to the Southern's chairman, who liked it and congratulated the young author/publisher.

This led to more titles covering the other main-line railways, as well as associated topics, and when the war ended IA decided to leave the Southern and go it alone. Which of course he did with notable success, first with booklets, books and magazines, and then building up a considerable empire which today includes car dealerships, a travel business, printing, property, bookshops and organic seeds. I suspect that many of today's transport enthusiasts were weaned on Ian Allan publications, whether underlining railway engine or bus numbers in the famous *ABC*s, or learning about buses in more depth in books and magazines. Certainly I started with railway *ABC*s before deciding that buses

were more interesting, so IA played an important part in moulding my subsequent career.

If R. Stuart Pilcher is a hero because of his time at Edinburgh Corporation, Moris Little is a hero because he not only guided the transport department in my native city for over 15 years, between 1948 and 1963, but also moved a short distance to become Chairman of the Scottish Bus Group, by then my employer. His name was on all of the city's buses — 'W. M. Little, Transport Manager' — so he was, as we say in Scotland, weel-kent (well-known) locally. His tenure at Edinburgh Corporation involved undoing much of Pilcher's work, as Moris Little pushed through the replacement of the trams with motorbuses, in line with several other municipalities.

Like John Rackham, Moris Little was a *Wunderkind*. He had been the youngest municipal manager, at St Helens and Reading, but had returned to his native Edinburgh in 1946 as Deputy Manager, stepping up two years later. The tram-replacement decision caused much local controversy, but Little was undaunted and the last trams ran in November 1956.

Little was well-travelled and was keen to bring Continental ideas to Edinburgh. First it was standee buses, which he bought in the early 1950s and which resurfaced a decade later in the still-familiar shape of three-door Leyland Leopard No 101. He also favoured lightweight construction, as evidenced by a fleet of well over 400 double-deckers

bought in a five-year period, each weighing well under 7 tons unladen. Indeed, it was In hls reign that the immortal words 'monstrous masses of shivering tin' were first used to describe the city's MCCW Orion-bodied Leyland PD2/20s.

At Scottish Bus Group, Little succeeded James Amos as Chairman. Amos had been with SMT since the mid-1920s and was an old-school intuitive hands-on busman. Moris Little was a different animal. He was a quiet, shy man, but more able to deal with an industry that was becoming more and more political as passenger numbers dropped and costs continued to rise. When he joined SBG it was still controlled from London by the Transport Holding Company, along with the Tilling group in England and Wales. When THC plus BET metamorphosed into the National Bus Company, he was guiding SBG back into Scottish control as the major part of the new Scottish Transport Group. Moris Little was not afraid to speak out when addressing the various professional bodies he supported, sounding alarm bells over the decline of the bus industry and predicting meltdown if it failed to get its act together.

I didn't have much contact with Moris Little at SBG — he was, after all, the Big White Chief —

but he was always prepared to listen to the hare-brained suggestions of keen youngsters out to change the world, and that counted for a lot. His contribution to transport in Scotland was great.

The same could — indeed can — be said of my final hero. For some of my senior colleagues at SBG, Brian Souter of Stagecoach was an irritation. How dare this young upstart run coaches to London in competition with us! For those of us in the middle tiers of management, however, here was an interesting and novel approach to running coaches — it was as if Brian had torn up the rule-book and started completely afresh. We watched him build up his coach business to London — though it's only fair to say that we invested in new coaches, cut fares and gave him a good run for his money.

We laughed as Souter took on our old adversaries at Strathclyde PTE with a fleet of Routemasters on some of the best corridors in

Above: **R. Stuart Pilcher (left) on Edinburgh's Last Tram night.** Gavin Booth collection

Left:**Brian Souter (centre) at the launch of the 'Megadekka', with Leyland salesmen Clive Hodgson (left) and Mike Ball.** Gavin Booth

Glasgow. And we watched open-mouthed as he bought Hampshire Bus and started on the acquisition trail. We also got to know him, because the Scottish bus world is not that big, and even competitors meet to talk and have a laugh together. And, yes, he did wear red shoes and carry his belongings in a carrier-bag — and probably still does.

The first time I interviewed Brian and his sister Ann, Stagecoach was already growing, with Cumberland, Hampshire Bus and United Counties under its belt, but their office — singular — was very basic, with room for two side-by-side desks and not much else. The story of Stagecoach's growth is well-known and probably already features in university business degree courses, but much of its success is a result of Brian's down-to-earth shrewdness; you have the feeling that he is really enjoying what he is doing, and his enthusiasm filters down to his staff.

Stagecoach undoubtedly took full advantage of bus deregulation and privatisation, but, if the world had stayed with regulation and state-ownership, I can't help feeling that Brian would still

be up there — perhaps as Managing Director of SBG or NBC. Now there's a thought... .

It would be misleading to pretend that the heroes I've listed are the only people I admire. There are others, of course — bus operators, manufacturers, even journalists — but their stories are for another time. (This paragraph is included for those who may have looked for their names in vain.)

And as for villains — oh, sorry, I've used up my allotted 2,784 words.

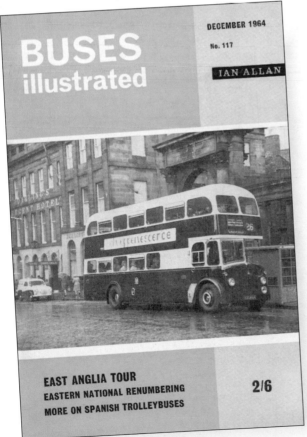

Left: **The December 1964 issue of** *Buses Illustrated,* **the first to feature a Gavin Booth photo on the cover.**
Ian Allan Library

Above: **Moris Little in Scottish Bus Group days.**
Gavin Booth collection

On the magazine cover:
BUSES illustrated
IAN ALLAN
DECEMBER 1964
No. 117
EAST ANGLIA TOUR
EASTERN NATIONAL RENUMBERING
MORE ON SPANISH TROLLEYBUSES
2/6

LEYLAND'S LYNX

Launched as the successor to the National, Leyland's Lynx was a victim of the changes sweeping through the British bus industry in the late 1980s. Now they are disappearing and many survivors look uncared for. Geoff Mills illustrates the Lynx in its heyday.

Above: This was the first complete production Lynx, a 51-seater with a Gardner engine. It was originally a Leyland demonstrator and then joined the fleet of West Riding. It is seen in Morley in 1992. The Lynx was built at Leyland's Workington plant and was originally offered with either a Leyland or a Gardner engine.

Right: This was another demonstrator, new in the spring of 1987 and sold to Jubilee Coaches of Stevenage later that year. It is seen in Stevenage in 1988 and already has a slightly down-at-heel look, with a replacement front nearside corner panel which hasn't been painted, and with diesel spillages staining the skirt.

Left: **Pan Atlas bought eight Lynxes with TL11 engines for operation on the company's first London bus contract. They entered service in the summer of 1988. This one is seen at Arnos Grove in March 1989.**

Below left: **Chambers of Bures bought this Cummins-engined Lynx in 1988 and ran it for almost 10 years. It was normally used in Sudbury, but once a week made the trip to Colchester, where it was photographed when new.**

Below: **Moor-Dale bought a pair of Lynxes at the end of 1987. In 1994 they were taken over by Northumbria, along with Moor-Dale's bus operations.**

Above: **A demonstrator with Cummins L10 engine was offered by Leyland in 1988/9 and is seen here on its first public outing at the 1988 Brighton Coach Rally. It was later sold to Cumberland Motor Services.**

Right: **Miller Bros of Foxton bought five Lynxes for park-and-ride contracts in Cambridge. All were taken over by Cambus in 1992.**

Below: **Shearings, best known for its coach operations, ran buses for a period after deregulation in 1986. It invested heavily in new Leylands, and these included 12 Lynxes in 1987/8. Eight passed to Yorkshire Traction in 1991, with the other four going to Maidstone & District.**

Above: **The London Borough of Hillingdon owned two Lynxes which operated on the 128. They were later purchased by London Buses. The registration mark matches the photographer's initials.**

Left: **In 1989 Sovereign Bus & Coach bought seven Lynxes, two of which are seen in the company's HertsRider livery in Stevenage in 1990.**

Top: **The Lynx II was launched at the end of 1990 and was offered with a Volvo engine, reflecting the new ownership of Leyland Bus, which had been bought by Volvo in 1988. The Lynx II was easily identifiable by its 'snout', designed to accommodate a revised cooling system. This demonstrator was operated by Tees & District in 1992, before being sold to Felix of Stanley at the end of that year.**

Above: **Another demonstrator with North East connections was this Lynx II which was bought by Cleveland Transit in 1992. It was one of relatively few Lynxes — 21, to be precise — to be built with a Volvo engine.**

Left: **Colchester Borough Transport's last Lynx — it had 14 — was this K-registered Mk II model. It entered service in September 1992, making it one of the last new Lynxes to take to the road, but only served in Colchester for two years before being moved to Crosville Wales following the purchase of CBT by British Bus.**

Left: Metrobus of Orpington bought this Lynx II from the Volvo Bus training school in August 1992. K-registered Lynxes were fairly rare, there being only 18 of them out of a total of just over 1,000 Lynxes built.

Below: With an eye on its business in Ulster, where the Alexander-bodied Bristol RE had been the favoured combination, Leyland offered Lynx underframes to Alexander's Belfast factory. Six (plus a prototype) were completed with Alexander N-type bodies for Ulsterbus and Citybus in 1985/6. All seven were bought by Stevensons of Uttoxeter in 1992.

PAISLEY
PATTERNS

Paisley has a long tradition of independent bus operation, and since deregulation in 1986 has attracted a large number of small operators. Billy Nicol illustrates a few.

Right: **McGill's Bus Service was an old-established family business, based in Barrhead, which sold out to Clydeside Buses in 1997. The McGill name survived the adoption of a corporate identity by Arriva, but faded away during 2000. This is a 1993 Dennis Dart with Plaxton Pointer body.**

Left: **Hutchison's of Renfrew started in 1991 and operated in Paisley until 1999, when it sold out to Arriva. This Freight Rover Sherpa was new to Crosville, and is seen in central Paisley in 1994.**

Above: **One of the shorter-lived operators running into Paisley in the mid-1990s was Quarriers of Bridge of Weir. Its fleet included this unusual Leyland Cub with HTI bodywork, which had been new to Westminster City Council.**

Left: **In 1992 Dickson's introduced a service from Paisley to Glasgow. Its fleet is made up of Mercedes minibuses, including this one with Plaxton Beaver 2 bodywork which came from a Preston operator.**

Above: **Dart Buses started in 1996 and has operated an interesting variety of new and second-hand buses. The latter include three DAF SB220s with Optare Delta bodywork — a rare sight north of the border — which were purchased from London United in 1999.**

Right: **Scotway launched a service between Paisley and Barrhead in 1999 using Mercedes minibuses. It briefly ran full-size buses, in the shape of Leyland Tigers with unusual Alexander P-type bodies which came from Stagecoach Fife. Operations soon reverted to Mercedes minis.**

Below right: **First Stop — started in 1991 as the Govan Minibus Co — links Paisley with Govan, using minibuses. These include this Plaxton-bodied Mercedes which was acquired from Sovereign Buses in 1999.**

Above: **Some idea of the 1990s minibus variety in Paisley can be seen in this line-up of an Iveco, a Renault and a Mercedes. The Iveco was operated by Bellview and carries the fleetname 'Bellview Buddie'; residents of Paisley are generally known as Buddies. This is the same location as the previous photograph, but before extension of the Piazza shopping centre.**

Above: **Marbill Travel — taking its name from founders Margaret and Bill — is based in Beith and operates a substantial school contract fleet. This Leyland Tiger with relatively unusual Plaxton Derwent bus body came from Travel West Midlands' Your Bus fleet. Marbill's bus livery is orange and cream, similar to that used by well-known Paisley operator Graham's Bus Service which closed in 1990.**

BIRMINGHAM
BLUES

Birmingham Corporation's blue-liveried buses were usually of distinctive design. Alan Broughall illustrates the fleet in the 1960s, when it was the country's biggest municipal bus operator with some 1,750 vehicles.

Left: **Among the first buses to carry the standard postwar Birmingham body were 75 AEC-engined Daimler CVA6s delivered in 1947. Their Metro-Cammell bodies seated 54. Subsequent Daimler deliveries had Daimler or Gardner engines. The CVA6s were withdrawn between 1961 and 1966.**

Below: **Birmingham's first Crossleys were 10 DD42/5s delivered in 1949. They had Crossley bodies which were generally similar to those built by Metro-Cammell, but with detail differences — the most obvious in this view is the shape of the side window under the staircase, which is almost a triangle. Note the timeclock in both this and the previous picture.**

Top left: In 1947 a batch of 15 RT-type AEC Regent IIIs joined the Birmingham fleet. These had 54-seat Park Royal bodies which had been built to resemble the Birmingham standard but used Park Royal's basic four-bay structure. The only other AEC double-decker to join the postwar Birmingham fleet was an ex-demonstration Bridgemaster in 1957.

Top right: This single Leyland-bodied PD2 Titan was purchased in 1947, but was followed by 200 PD2s between 1948 and 1950 with bodies by Brush (100), Park Royal (50) and Leyland (50).

Above left: The Brush-bodied PD2s were built to Birmingham's design, which looked rather old-fashioned when compared with the standard Leyland body. Good eyesight was needed to read three lines of print in a destination box which was little deeper than that used for a single place-name by most other fleets.

Above right: Single-deckers played a small part in Birmingham's operations at the start of the 1960s, and its only postwar half-cabs were 30 Tiger PS2/1s with 34-seat Weymann bodies, delivered in 1950. These were long-lived buses, most surviving until 1968, by which time urban half-cab single-deckers were a rare sight.

Above: Birmingham pioneered the use of the double-deck Daimler Fleetline chassis as the basis for a single-decker, taking 24 in 1965 for use on a route with a 10ft height restriction. The 37-seat bodies were by Marshall. In the days before the National Lottery, a £25,000 premium-bond win was considered a fortune.

Right: Later Birmingham standard bodies featured top-sliding sections to the side windows, as on this 1952 Daimler CVG6 bodied by Crossley. It is unusual in having been rebuilt with a Manchester-style glass-fibre bonnet and grille in place of the standard Birmingham 'new look' front.

Below right: Although Birmingham Corporation became a major Fleetline buyer, its first rear-engined bus was this 1960 Leyland Atlantean; it was operated as a demonstrator in the autumn of that year, and then purchased in the spring of 1961 along with 10 similar buses. It was the first front-entrance bus in the fleet, and had a 71-seat Metro-Cammell body. Note the simplified livery.